KU-355-222

MAP OF
BRITAIN IN THE
DARK AGES

COVER DESIGN

The main feature of the cover design is the Vendel-style helmet found in the East Anglian royal ship-burial at Sutton Hoo, Suffolk, in 1939, and now in the British Museum. This reconstruction has been carried out by the Archaeology Division of the Ordnance Survey in consultation with the Department of British and Medieval Antiquities, British Museum. Modifications in shape and detail occur in this, the first attempted reconstruction in colour, as compared with the helmet as hitherto published or as at present seen in the British Museum. These modifications include the size of the crown, the angle at which the visor is set, and the size of the eye openings; rearrangement of the figure and interlace panels on the crown; and the transposition of the dragon heads, of different design, which terminate the crest. While every effort has been made to achieve accuracy, this drawing is not to be regarded as definitive; and in particular it is possible that the panels of interlace on the visor were originally tinned, and not gilded as shown in this reconstruction.

£1·30

ARCHAEOLOGICAL & HISTORICAL MAPS

Since its early years the Ordnance Survey has been concerned with investigating, recording and surveying the archaeology of the country. This work is aimed at ensuring that archaeological features are shown correctly on the standard maps, but over the years it has been possible to collate and categorise the information and publish it in the form of special archaeological and historical maps. These maps with their explanatory texts have made a valuable contribution to the knowledge of the country's past in the periods and subjects which have been covered in the series.

The maps are of three types:

1. General Maps (dealing with specific periods or cultures)

Southern Britain in the Iron Age.
Roman Britain.
Britain in the Dark Ages.
Britain before the Norman Conquest.

2. Thematic Maps (showing the distribution and character of certain features).

Ancient Britain.
Monastic Britain.

3. Individual Monuments

Hadrian's Wall.
The Antonine Wall.

Map Catalogue

Full details of these maps and of "Field Archaeology in Great Britain" which contains information and advice on all aspects of field archaeology, are given in the Ordnance Survey catalogue which is available free on request to the Ordnance Survey, Romsey Road, Maybush, Southampton SO9 4DH.

MAP OF BRITAIN

in the

DARK AGES

Second Edition

SCALE

Sixteen Miles to One Inch

Made and published by the

DIRECTOR GENERAL OF THE ORDNANCE SURVEY

SOUTHAMPTON

© CROWN COPYRIGHT

1966

Text reprinted with corrections 1974

CONTENTS

FOREWORD

This is the Second Edition of a map of Britain in the Dark Ages which originally appeared in two sheets at the scale of 1:1,000,000, North and South, in 1939 and 1935 respectively. The most obvious change now made is the adoption of a single sheet form covering the whole of Great Britain at the same scale.

Much progress has been made in Dark Age studies since 1935 and a comparison of the two versions will show that there have been many additions. Some of these are to categories of features already dealt with on the first edition and others are new. An example of novelty is the application of more than one hundred and fifty early monastic sites to the map. Another innovation is the showing of the whole known Roman road system as a background feature wherever it occurs. Although it went into decline rapidly in the fifth century its influence on the development of Anglo-Saxon settlement cannot be ignored.

We have had the advantage of using the late Dr. V.E. Nash Williams' great study of early Christian monuments in Wales which was still in an early stage in 1935. In most respects this map follows closely on the pioneering work of the late Dr. O.G.S. Crawford who laid its foundations so firmly in 1935 and 1939. The need for economy has led to the abandonment of certain embellishments which appeared on the first edition, but this has in no way impaired the usefulness of the map. The introduction has been completely re-written and an index is supplied which categorises all the main classes of Dark Age antiquity, ranges them in alphabetical order and supplies full details of their location.

The whole of the compilation has been the work of the former Archaeology Officer, Mr. C.W. Phillips, O.B.E., M.A., F.S.A., who acknowledges the assistance of scholars and archaeologists in many parts of the country, too numerous to be mentioned individually by name here. A particular debt is owed to Mr. C.A. Ralegh Radford, M.A., D.LITT.,F.B.A.,F.S.A., whose advice has been valuable at all stages of the work, to Professor Kenneth Jackson, M.A., LITT.D., D.LITT.CELT., F.B.A., of the University of Edinburgh for help with names and to Mr. R.B.K. Stevenson, M.A., F.S.A., the Director of the National Museum of Antiquities of Scotland, Edinburgh, for counsel on Scottish problems.

I would like to offer the thanks of the Department, both on my own behalf and on that of my predecessor Major-General A.H. Dowson, C.B., C.B.E., under whom the bulk of the work was carried out, to these and to all others who have freely given of their time and knowledge to help bring this work to completion.

(R. C. A. EDGE)
Major-General,
Director General.

INTRODUCTION

This is the first revision of the *Map of Britain in the Dark Ages* produced by Dr. O.G.S. Crawford and issued by the Ordnance Survey in two parts in 1935 and 1939. As a description of the period under review (410 - 871) the term "Dark Ages" grows less appropriate with the advance of knowledge, but alternatives such as "Migration and Early Medieval Period", which have gained currency elsewhere, though possibly more precise, are cumbersome and the older name still contains much truth — as any compiler must know from bitter experience. The title has therefore been kept unchanged.

The scale of the original map (1:1,000,000 or 16 miles to the inch) has also been retained, but the whole of Great Britain is now treated on one sheet. The earlier division into two sheets had something to commend it, since the evidence for the period differs considerably both in quality and quantity in Northern and Southern Britain. Scotland has nothing equivalent to the Anglo-Saxon Chronicle to provide a continuous narrative and, save for the lengthy episode of the unsuccessful Northumbrian attempt to subdue the Pictish kingdom and various ecclesiastical contacts, the affairs of the north and south are largely distinct. Similarly the dates at which it is convenient to open and close the treatment of the southern region have no particular significance in the north. The union of the Picts and Scots under Kenneth mac Alpin, which occurred *c.*850, may be considered as a general terminal date in Scotland, but it cannot be applied with any rigidity since certain important features of Pictish art, in decline after this date, continue to appear until the end of the 9th century. On the other hand the divided treatment was only made possible by a substantial overlap between the two sheets, allowing the country between Hadrian's Wall and the Forth-Clyde isthmus to appear on both. On historical and economic grounds alike there is great convenience to the user in providing one map to cover the whole of Great Britain.

This map is concerned to show the present state of knowledge and to provide an index of progress in the study of a period which is still full of perplexities and empty places. Most of our information about Pagan Anglo-Saxon England continues to come from archaeological sources depending heavily on the contents of cemeteries, though some important progress has recently been made in piecing together various items which increase our knowledge of early Anglo-Saxon life. Dark Age Scotland is a difficult subject, and much of what appears on this map does more to define where some work has been done rather than to give a properly balanced picture of the time. Much remains to be done, but we can see the serious gaps in our knowledge. Experience has shown that this visual demonstration is one of the most useful functions of Ordnance Survey period maps which thus act as guides and stimuli to further work.

The new map differs from its predecessor in two obvious respects. Britain was covered with the structural features of the Roman provinces when our period begins in 410 and these were bound to have some influence on the new dispensation even though much was ruined, ignored and rejected by the Anglo-Saxons in the stage of settlement. It has therefore been thought desirable to show the skeleton of the defunct provinces by indicating the Roman road system by pecked lines. The second change is seen in the abandonment of any attempt to restore natural woodlands on a geological basis. No apology is due for this. It has already been done on the third edition of the map of Roman Britain because wider knowledge of human distribution in that period shows that most of the naturally wooded areas carried much larger populations than was thought possible thirty years ago. Specific instances are the lands bordering on the Great Ouse and Warwickshire Avon which constitute a belt across the Midlands, and a greater density of Romano-British settlement can now be recognised in most of these areas. In any case the ancient equipment for cutting and removing timber was not greatly different from that which was commonly used in this country until as late as the 18th century. Many natural woodlands are on good soil and this was recognised long before our period began. Great woodlands remained in our period and no doubt there was some local re-establishment of scrub and forest in the 5th and 6th centuries, but it is unlikely to have been a major factor affecting settlement at this time. Our first real information about the full extent of woodlands in Anglo-Saxon times does not come till the Domesday Survey of 1086. Where there is much uncertainty the need to clarify a map which must carry much detail is a sufficient justification for the omission of woodlands.

Space does not permit the full discussion of the relations between the dying Roman province and its enemies in the 5th century. The Roman army and civil officials departed leaving the Romano-Britons to their own devices. A form of government by a group of *civitates* carried on to mid-century with the occasional help of people like St. Germanus of Auxerre till the failure of the appeal to Aetius in 446 was probably a final blow to its credit. Thereafter begins the rise of the sub-Roman tyrants we read of in Gildas. Saxons were already among those enemies repulsed by St. Germanus in 429. They were now introduced as mercenaries settled in the land to aid in its defence. The break-down of the relations between these and the tyrants was followed by more arrivals from overseas and a struggle began which was sustained on the British side by leaders like Ambrosius Aurelianus and the enigmatic Arthur. By *c.*500 when they had won the battle of Mons Badonicus the Britons were holding their own. Many of the invaders withdrew to the Continent and when Gildas wrote the country was at peace, though large areas remained under Anglo-Saxon control.

The problem of Romano-British survival in the areas of primary Anglo-Saxon settlement remains unsolved. There may have been enclaves lasting for some time in areas like the Fenland, the Chilterns and, further west, in the Isle of Purbeck and elsewhere, but the archaeological evidence for these, at least, is at present negligible. The surviving elements of the Romano-British population in the East, South-east and Midlands have left us no signs of their presence which are clearly recognisable today. Certainly none of them can be expressed in cartographic terms and the situation is little better in the West outside Devon, Cornwall and Wales. Most of the major Roman towns come up again out of the twilight of these centuries, but there are notable casualties which barely recover village status. In some areas the pattern shifts; thus Reading succeeds Silchester, Shrewsbury takes the place of Wroxeter and Hereford follows on from Kenchester through the hard facts of local topography asserting themselves.

The decay of the road system must have been early and severe when bridges broke, engineering works failed and major arteries lay for long in debatable lands. No doubt the degree of decay varied from place to place, but its havoc among roads which were seldom better than roughly macadamised surfaces may be imagined by noting how swiftly an abandoned piece of modern tar macadam can be broken up by the forces of weather and vegetation. Even more to the point is the astonishingly quick return to nature of recently-abandoned railway tracks whose road beds have been laid thick with hard materials and consolidated by a century of train traffic. We may marvel that so many traces of the Roman road system remain to us.

We may also recall that in at least two places on major Roman roads Anglo-Saxons buried many of their dead full in the carriage way. This may be a local aberration, but it suggests that often the Roman road system survived as an indication of routes to be followed across country between slowly-reviving centres of population rather than as continuous surfaces still usable over long distances.

THE USE OF COLOUR

Three colours are used in the overprint on this map, black, red and blue. During the period under review two worlds, Celtic and Germanic, are confronting each other in Britain, and the adoption of Christianity by the Anglo-Saxons only mitigates and does not resolve this conflict.

Symbols representing features belonging to the Celtic world are shown in *blue*. On the Germanic side *black* is used for the pagan phase and *red* for everything belonging to the Conversion and its consequences. In general the two main distributions are well separated and overlapping only occurs in limited areas like parts of Southern Scotland. *Black* is also used for symbols indicating towns and more important inhabited places, battle sites, and all names.

THE HISTORICAL SCOPE OF THE MAP

ENGLAND

This map covers the whole of the formative period of the Anglo-Saxon settlement up to the accession of Alfred to the throne of Wessex in 871. Although it contains many obscure places, particularly in its first hundred and fifty years, the general course of early Anglo-Saxon history is sufficiently clear and it will be enough here to mention the crucial phases in the establishment of Anglo-Saxon rule over England.

During this period the original inhabitants of what had been Roman Britain were subjected to a steady pressure which left Wales as the only independent British region south of the Solway. How much this process owes to Teutonic federates already settled as mercenaries in the 4th and 5th centuries and how much to fresh bands of immigrants cannot be considered here. Obviously the latter were the more considerable in number. The details remain a matter of contention but the contest with the Britons certainly had its changes of fortune. At the close of the 5th century the struggle was being maintained on something like equal terms, and the British victory at Mons Badonicus *c*.500 repulsed the westward advance of the Saxons for at least a generation. But although there is evidence that some Saxons withdrew from Britain altogether under the stress of this defeat their general hold on the East and South-east of the country was not relinquished. The nucleus of the kingdom of Wessex in the Middle Thames valley remained and began to expand once more after victories at Old Sarum in 552 and at Bedcanford in 571. These led to penetration into Wiltshire resulting in the outflanking of Dorset and the subjugation of a wide belt of country in the south Midlands. Then a decisive blow was struck when Ceawlin won the battle of Deorham in 577 and seized the old Roman centres at Gloucester, Cirencester and Bath. This brought the West Saxons to the lower Severn on a broad front and drove a wedge between the Britons of Wales and those of the South-west. A large exodus of the latter to Brittany and the Loire Valley eased the way for a steady Saxon penetration into Devon and Eastern Cornwall accompanied by extensive settlement, which began with the battle of Bindon in 614. The conquest of the South-west was finally completed by Egbert at the battle of Hingston Down in 838.

In the north of England the 6th century saw the beginning of the Anglian kingdom of Northumbria. Its southern part, Deira, may originate from a take-over by Germanic mercenaries, but its real nucleus was the Bernician coastal fortress of Bamburgh, the point of settlement of a war band under Ida in 547. In the next fifty years the British reaction to this Anglian intrusion was so sharp that the invaders made little progress inland from the coast, but although Urien of Rheged is said to have driven the newcomers back into Lindisfarne for a time, a Bernician victory over the North Welsh at Catterick confirmed their hold. The accession of Ethelfrith to the throne of Bernicia in 593 heralded a strong advance. A still unbroken stretch of country held by various British princi-palities, Rheged, Elmet and Strathclyde, extended from the general area of North Wales to the Forth-Clyde line, and most of the Pennines were in their control. Ethelfrith began the offensive in 616 by defeating the British king of Powys at Chester. It is not clear how far this carried the Angles per-manently to the coast of Lancashire, but it began the separation of the Britons of Wales from those of Strathclyde, a similar disruptive effect to that of the battle of Deorham on the South-west. In 603 Ethelfrith also gave a severe check to the expansion of the new Scotic kingdom of Dalriada by defeating Aedán mac Gabráin at Degsastan somewhere in the region of the later Border. Ethelfrith then took over Deira and Northumbria was born. After Ethelfrith's death in battle Edwin of Deira, who had been driven into exile, seized the whole kingdom and the Bernician family sought refuge in Dalriada, coming into contact with Celtic Christianity at Iona with important consequences for the future. Edwin continued the pressure against the North Welsh with some success and the Celtic kingdoms of Rheged and Elmet now lost their independence, but a new factor appeared when the Angles of the north and west Midlands coalesced to form Mercia. Meanwhile Edwin had accepted Christianity in its Latin form from Paulinus. An alliance of the new Mercian power under Penda with Cadwallon of Wales led to Edwin's defeat and death at Hatfield Chase in 632. Northumbria was severely ravaged and fell back into its constituent parts for a while, but the Britons had pushed to the North Sea for the last time because in 633 Oswald, the Bernician king returned from exile, defeated and slew Cadwallon near Hexham and restored Northumbria.

Thus within thirty years, and in spite of several reversals of fortune, the British world of the West had been split into three parts. The south-western fragment was destined to wither away in the next two hundred years and the Strathclyde Britons were to fall back deep into Scotland. These events were decisive for the Anglo-Saxon domination of England.

By the end of the 7th century Northumbria had reached and passed the summit of its political power. An expansion far into Scotland ended with the defeat and death of Ecgfrith at the hands of the Picts at Nechtansmere in 685 and his earlier defeat by the Mercians on the Trent in 674 had begun a period of Mercian supremacy which culminated in the reign of Offa, Charlemagne's contemporary, the first Anglo-Saxon king who can be regarded as a European figure and the only serious rival of Alfred as a great ruler.

The attacks of the Northmen finally ruined Northumbria, struck down Mercia and carried the supremacy to Wessex in the successful reign of Egbert, Alfred's grandfather.

This brings us to the close of our period. A number of the smaller kingdoms of the early days had been swallowed up in the larger combinations. The political unity of the country was still to be achieved but it was now unlikely that any British revival could shake the hold of the Anglo-Saxons. The real challenge came from overseas and the period closes as the kingdom of Wessex braces itself for a desperate struggle for survival against the Northmen.

Christianity came to the Anglo-Saxons from different directions and in different traditions. As Bede complained, the Britons made no attempt to convert their enemies. The mission of Augustine in 597 brought Latin Christianity to the South-east whence it was soon carried by Paulinus and James the Deacon into Northumbria, but there it had to meet the challenge of the Celtic form which had come in with the returning exile Oswald. The missionary activity of the Celtic monks was intense but the Latins had powerful champions in Theodore of Tarsus, Benedict Biscop and Wilfrid. The victory of the Latin church was secured by the synod of Whitby in 663, a crucial event in Anglo-Saxon history because it directed the new England into the current of Latin civilisation with incalculable effects on its ideas and institutions.

WALES

By the end of our period in 871 Wales was the only surviving independent British region of Southern Britain and carried on its own life west of Offa's Dyke which had defined its frontier with Mercia for nearly one hundred years past. The story of Wales from the 5th century onwards was affected by more than the clash of Celt and Saxon. At the close of the Roman period both the north and the south of the country was the scene of important immigrations from Ireland as well as the episode of the coming of Cunedda from the Lowlands of Scotland to found the dynasty which was to rule long in North Wales. South Wales as far east as the borders of Brechiniog and Erging was strongly affected by Irish settlers from South-east Ireland whose original function may have been to defend it against others of their own kin. It is clear that for some time before the end of the 4th century the defence of Wales as a whole was ceasing to be the task of formal Roman forces and was becoming the concern of the natives, though far more work will have to be done among the old fortresses surviving from pre-Roman times before the full character and extent of this will be apparent.

The feature of life in Dark Age Wales which is most easily shown on a map today is the evidence for Christianity. This chiefly takes the form of a large number of monuments—memorial stones, early crosses, etc.—which are found freely everywhere except in Central Wales and have their heaviest concentration in the south. While these give evidence of a feebly surviving Romanity influenced from contemporary Gaul they also attest the influence of the Irish both in their form and their inscriptions.

The secular side of life is not so clear. Much work has been done in recent years in trying to sort out the various types of hut settlement which are current from Bronze Age times right through the Roman period into the Dark Ages, but there does not seem to be any clear-cut change in their form marking the passage into post-Roman times. The only certain criterion of Dark Age date is the finding of material clearly belonging to this period in a site, and the limited amount of excavation which has taken place makes it impossible to point to more than a handful of sites where this dating has been securely established. Thus any cartographic treatment of this subject is more of a map of work done than any true distribution pattern. Something more can now be done to show the principal religious centres, monastic and otherwise, than was possible twenty-five years ago, but that is all. Some hope of better things has been given recently by the results of excavating the home of a minor Welsh chief at Dinas Powys near Cardiff.

SCOTLAND

Southern Britain has many written and archaeological sources from which a reasonably well stocked map of its Dark Age topography can be compiled, but North Britain is not so fortunate. The sources for the period there are few, indifferent in quality, and often second hand. The certain archaeological evidence does not go far beyond the surviving works of Pictish and Scotic art.

At the opening of the 5th century it is probably safe to say that all North Britain beyond the Forth-Clyde line was essentially Pictish. This was soon modified by the rise of the intrusive Scotic kingdom of Dalriada in Argyll and the neighbouring islands. This realm may be regarded as the most significant result of the various raids which had been made by the Irish against Western Britain in the 4th and 5th centuries. They failed to have any permanent effect in England and Wales. This new power in Argyll sprang from Irish Dalriada, the area now known as Northern Antrim. Its traditional founders *c.*500 were Fergus, son of Erc, and his brothers Loarn and Angus. Some dependence on the Irish homeland seems to have survived until the time of Aedán mac Gabráin (*c.*574 - 608). He was an aggressive ruler who extended his sway over the Pictish lands between Forth and Tay, but when he turned south he was decisively repulsed by Ethelfrith of Bernicia at Degsastan in 603. This check in the political sphere was to last for some time, but the arrival of St. Columba from Ireland and the founding of Iona in 563 made Dalriada a vital source of Christian influence in the Irish style which was to have a powerful effect upon the evangelisation of Northern and much of Southern Britain. The principal strongholds of the new kingdom were at Dunadd in the Moss of Crinan and Dunollie near Oban.

South-western Scotland was occupied by the Brittonic realm of Strathclyde whose origins probably go back to the 5th century. It had varying fortunes and much of its southern part in the regions of Rheged and Galloway fell under Northumbrian control by the 7th century, but its final extinction as a political entity did not take place until after our period closed. At the eastern end of the Forth-Clyde isthmus was the region of Manau Guotodin, the land of the Votadini, covering Lothian and most of the Eastern Lowlands. This had its origin before the 5th century began. We have already seen that Scotic influence in this area was threatened by the defeat at Degsastan and this was followed by a Northumbrian penetration as far as the Forth, of which we have no details, but which certainly ended the separate existence of Manau Guotodin. This deep intrusion of Anglian Northumbria permanently affected the eastern half of the Lowlands with important long-term consequences for the historic kingdom of Scotland, but for the time being a long period of friction between the Picts and the Northumbrians began.

Thus the early years of the 7th century found Northumbria and the Pictish power as the only immediate contenders for the whole of the eastern part of North Britain. Northumbria was subject to sudden changes of fortune through her relations with the Welsh and the rising kingdom of Mercia in the South, but by the time of Oswiu in the mid-7th century it appears that Fife and even part of Angus were being disputed with the Picts. An attempt was made to place a seal of permanency on the Northumbrian advance by founding the see of Abercorn in 681. But the scene changed with dramatic suddenness when Ecgfrith, pressing too far into Angus, was defeated and slain by Brude mac Beli at Nechtansmere in 685. This set a term to Northumbrian expansion in the North. The Forth did not cease to be the frontier between Northumbria and Pictland in general, but the Picts recovered the lands they had lost north of it, and the overlordship which the Northumbrians had imposed on the Scots and the Strathclyde Britons came to an end along with the see of Abercorn. Nechtansmere was decisive and a series of dynastic disputes and wars with Mercia prevented any more large Northumbrian enterprises in North Britain. Even so Northumbria continued to dominate most of the Lowlands until she herself was struck down by the Northmen in 867. After the union of the Picts and Scots Lothian passed more and more under Scottish influence and the no man's land of the North shifted south from the Forth-Clyde line to the present Border where it was to remain till the 17th century.

The Picts have long been a mysterious factor in the early history of North Britain, but much of the fantasy and conjecture which have surrounded them has been stripped away by a recent publication, *The Problem of the Picts* (Nelson, Edinburgh, 1955.) Here they begin to appear in their true light as the political combination of various elements living in East and North Scotland in late Roman times. It is unknown whether there was a single Pictish kingdom as early as 550, but by 565 when St. Columba made his famous journey to convert Brude mac Maelchon, ruler of the Northern Picts, near Inverness, there is a strong suggestion that there were two combinations, the Northern and Southern Picts, the latter occupying all Eastern Scotland north of the Forth as far as Banffshire. The rest of North Scotland fell to the Northern Picts who also exercised some control over the Orkneys and Shetlands. A hundred years after Columba's mission the two areas seem to have been united under one rule or overlordship, but the character of the territory and its traditions probably made this unity superficial and liable to easy disturbance. In the 7th century the Picts were ruled by a variety of kings with mixed Irish, British, Anglian and native descents due to much intermarriage among the northern royal houses. Under strong rule the Picts were formidable and capable of vigorous action on land and sea. Many surviving sculptures testify to their powers as artists and there were learned men among them; it is unfortunate that no Pictish literature has survived. Their union with the kingdom of Dalriada under Kenneth mac Alpin *c.*850 dissolves their identity and merges it in the Scottish people of history.

In all this we have little that we can show on a map with any certainty. The battle of Degsastan, though placed at Dawston in Liddesdale with considerable probability, is not certainly located and the site of Nechtansmere has only recently been placed beyond doubt by F.T. Wainwright. Abercorn we can place, and the find spots of those few material evidences of the Northumbrian period in the Lowlands which have survived, chiefly crosses. On the side of the Scots there are certain strongholds, some religious sites and monuments, but little more. It is only in Pictland that a considerable body of evidence survives in the form of symbol stones, crosses, and a few portable objects. The Picts were clearly a gifted people whose cultural level, at its best, was probably little inferior to that of most of the rest of Britain, but neither they nor their western enemies, the Scots, have left any written record to equal the Anglo-Saxon Chronicle or the works of Bede. Indeed it is from the latter that we get much of the information about them that we possess, or else from other external compilations like the Annals of Ulster.

Christianity came early to North Britain, but we know of nothing before the 5th century. If we are to believe Bede and some collateral evidence the Southern Picts were converted by St. Ninian's mission in the first half of the 5th century. The pagan cemeteries of Anglo-Saxon England pose many problems which await answers, but they do give us valuable topographic evidence of the general siting of the new settlements and of the progressive stages of the Germanic expansion in Southern Britain. In this connection it is worth recalling that our knowledge of early Northumbria, and particularly of the Northumbrian advance to the Forth and into South-west Scotland, would be almost non-existent if we relied on the evidence of cemeteries because at most of the material times the Northumbrians were Christians. In default of literary evidence place names would be our only guide. The whole of North Britain has little to show beyond the long cist cemeteries which cluster thickly on both sides of the Forth and a few uncertain records of the association of Pictish symbol stones with burials. Thus funerary evidence is not very helpful, and it is only on general probability rather than on any secure evidence that even these cemeteries are shown on the map.

Defensive structures provide a similar situation. At present early Anglo-Saxon works are confined to linear earthworks and the recognition of enclosed defences is only just beginning, but the age of most of these linear earthworks is in no doubt. In North Britain there are many forts which must have been active right through our period. Some are mentioned in history and so are placed on the map, but many more are unclassified for want of archaeological evidence and must await proper recognition. Small finds also give little help and the secure identification of contemporary dwellings is difficult. The distribution of distinctive objects like the Pictish silver chains is not spread equally over the whole Pictish area but is mainly confined to its southern verge and beyond. Thus it may be no more than a reflection of the conflicts between Picts and Northumbrians. Hoards are few and the most striking example which certainly belongs to the period has come from far north in the Shetlands.

Scotland contains notable relics of early Christianity today. First in time, if not in artistic merit, are those which can plausibly be associated with the mission of St. Ninian. The traces of his work extend southwards into Cumbria as well as over Southern Scotland. It is possible to see signs of his activity as far north as Skye in the west and into Southern Pictland and it is conceivable that the long cist cemeteries have something to do with this mission, but it is still too early to see his influence spreading as far as the Northern Islands. There is, however, no reason to doubt Bede's view that St. Ninian was responsible for the first evangelisation of much of Southern and Eastern Scotland, and his labours were continued for two hundred years by notable successors from St. Caranoc in the mid-5th century, through St. Donnan the Great who was martyred in 618, on to St. Walloch in the early 8th century. St. Ninian's monastic house at Whithorn exercised a powerful influence in Ireland as well as in Scotland and its independence was only extinguished when the tide of Northumbrian conquest poured over into Galloway and the Anglian bishopric of Whithorn was set up in the early 8th century.

Scotland was to be the scene of many missionary labours in the period following St. Ninian. Some were directed mainly to the west and north-west while others affected Pictland, but practically all had their origin in Ireland. There are many famous names, St. Brendan, St. Kentigern, St. Finnan, St. Blaan, St. Ronan, St. Moluag and St. Maelrubha, but none equalled in fame and importance

St. Columba who founded his house at Iona in 563. In his political influence he was a strong supporter of his Dalriadic kinsmen and his importance as one of the founders of Scotland is in no doubt. But it is difficult to illustrate many of these activities on this map. The association of various saints with a limited number of places is certain, but the use of church dedications as a guide to their movements is unsound and has been rejected. The map can do little more than show a limited number of famous sites like Iona, Lismore, Kingarth and Applecross along with some cashels and crosses. The coming decades will no doubt see a much closer scrutiny of the field archaeology of early Christianity in North Britain with fruitful results.

RECENT PROGRESS IN THE ARCHAEOLOGY OF BRITAIN IN THE DARK AGES

The last twenty years have seen marked progress in our understanding of the archaeology of this period, some details of which will be given under separate heads below. Any wider knowledge of conditions in 5th century Britain comes very slowly. The high lights here are some surprising discoveries prolonging the life of Roman St. Albans and various finds in hill forts in Wales tending to confirm some of the traditions of this period. But Arthurian Britain continues to be elusive. A better understanding of the scale of life at the top level of Anglo-Saxon society has been given by some fortunate discoveries like the Sutton Hoo ship burial, Edwin of Northumbria's residence at Yeavering and the Wessex royal manor at Cheddar. These have confirmed the testimony of early poets and opened up new vistas. At a lower level there has been an advance in systematic studies over most of the field. Pagan Anglo-Saxon cemeteries have been examined with more thoroughness and objectivity. Some major linear earthworks have been reconsidered with striking results, but settlement sites remain in short supply. The first large timber dwelling houses of Anglo-Saxon date have now been found. A beginning has been made with the recognition and study of closed defensive works, but perhaps the most hopeful development has been an expanding knowledge of all forms of Anglo-Saxon pottery both in its Continental affinities in the early days and in its local developments round England after the pagan period. The archaeology of any post-Mesolithic period in Western Europe can only be well founded on a good knowledge of the pottery types and sequences which are normally the commonest type fossils of its various phases. When Crawford produced the first edition of this map, knowledge of pagan Anglo-Saxon pottery in this country was elementary and that of the later period down to the 11th century almost non-existent. This is now ended. Much remains to be done, but the work of J.N.L. Myres, G.C. Dunning, E.M. Jope, and J.G. Hurst has laid the foundations of a complete system for pottery in Southern Britain between the collapse of the Roman province and the coming of the Normans.

Nor has the Celtic West and North been behindhand in this question of pottery types. Much of the material which has to be considered seems to have been imported and the quantities are small, but a beginning is being made with the recognition of wheel-made wares of sub-Roman character, presumably made in the western and northern parts of Southern Britain at least as late as 450 and possibly fifty years later. This has come from Dinas Powys near Cardiff, four sites in Cornwall and two in Scotland. In due course kilns may be found as the wares are technically similar to earlier Romano-British wares.

Imported pottery seems to have come from two main sources, the Eastern Mediterranean and the neighbouring Gaulish and Frankish lands. In the case of the Mediterranean wares some can be described as domestic, but the bulk of the material comes from large containers of amphora type in which wine was imported. These have been found in Ireland, Cornwall, Devon, Wales and, less certainly, in Western Scotland. When due allowance is made for our ignorance of anything like the full distribution of this pottery it seems probable that the amounts involved were never large and that the contact with the Mediterranean world was occasional and tenuous. It cannot have survived the Arab conquest of North Africa which closed the straits of Gibraltar when Arab power was extended into Spain early in the 8th century at a time when Devon and Cornwall were finally coming under the suzerainty of Wessex. Some doubt has recently been expressed about the date of this importation of Mediterranean wares with the suggestion that it really belongs to the 4th and early 5th centuries, thus falling within the Roman period.

The wares presumed to come from Gaul have a wider distribution. While there is little trace of the Mediterranean material in the north, the western and northern areas are affected by this pottery from nearer home and in some cases glass wares from the Merovingian lands accompanied it. Beginning in the early 5th century its importation probably continued until the swing of Rhenish trade to the southern and eastern ports of Britain brought it to an end in the 8th century.

There is also one locally produced pottery to be considered. This is the so-called "grass-marked" ware which at present has a purely Cornish distribution on this side of the Irish Sea. This may be another result of the Irish movement into Western Britain, but so far none of this pottery has been found north of the Bristol Channel though, as an Irish trait, it ought to occur in South Wales. As the study of the implications of all these wares occurring in Western and Northern Britain is obviously still in its early stages our presentation of their distribution on the map is provisional.

Finally, in the Anglo-Saxon field there has been much critical re-examination of early church architecture and excavations have increased our knowledge of the details of early monasteries at Whitby, Glastonbury, Tintagel and Burgh Castle. The examination of bomb-damaged towns has also begun to throw some light on the beginning of Anglo-Saxon town life.

ANGLO-SAXON TOWNS

During this period town life reached its lowest ebb in historic times and little progress has yet been made towards solving the problem of how much of it survived into the 6th century. No clear evidence has come to light of any effective occupation of Roman town sites by pagan Anglo-Saxons in the area of primary settlement in the later 5th century, though there are sometimes indications that they were living close by.

The last stage in the life of Roman towns is not easily recoverable, partly because of the disturbance of the latest levels by the re-use of the sites, and partly from the difficulty of recognising its traces when they consist of no more than small finds. But there is no reason to suppose that any heavy disasters had befallen most Roman towns before 450 and some confirmation of this fact has recently come to light at St. Albans. Here fairly substantial buildings were still being put up in the middle of the Roman town in the first half of the 5th century and evidence of continuing organisation is shown by the finding of a wooden water pipe line which can hardly have been placed in position before 450. We are reminded that St. Germanus of Auxerre was able to meet a magistrate called *vir tribuniciae potestatis* in charge of St. Albans in 429. There is no need to expect any major collapse of the towns in the eastern half of the country until after the revolt of the Teutonic mercenaries which is indicated by the story of Hengist and Horsa. Gildas attributes the ruin of towns to this phase, but we do not know the extent of the areas affected by the wars of the later 5th century before the British victory of Mons Badonicus *c.*500; there are a number of Roman towns in the West and South-west which may have been able to carry on some semblance of Roman life until half-way through the 6th century unless they chanced to be destroyed in raids. Some evidence of late survival has been found at Venta Silurum (Caerwent) in an area which, at this stage, had more to fear from the Irish than the Saxons, but fairly extensive excavations in Roman Exeter suggest that urban life was already at a low ebb there as early as 400. The work now in progress at Cirencester and Winchester may throw more light on this problem. When at last town life ceased the essentially rural pattern of Anglo-Saxon life postponed any revival for a long time. But knowledge of the old towns persisted. Some degree of travel must have continued along the lines of the Roman roads. These, if used at all, led to the sites of towns which in many cases were only waiting to begin a slow recovery.

The arrival of the Augustinian mission in Southern Britain did little to promote the growth of towns in its early days. In the North and wherever the Celtic missionaries made their way, town life received no encouragement because the urban tradition was foreign to all but one, Ninian, and he has left no mark in this field. Augustine, Paulinus and Theodore of Tarsus came from Mediterranean lands where town life was more vigorous, but they arrived too late to revive it in Britain in their own life times. Gregory the Great was responsible for Augustine's mission and hoped to organise the new branch of the Church from urban centres. Two metropolitan sees were to be established at Canterbury and York with twelve other bishoprics dependent on each. The sees were to be sited so that communication might be easy; the use of town sites was clearly implied and the general plan was based on the contemporary division of Anglo-Saxondom between the Southern English and Northumbria. The original intention to move the centre of the southern province from Canterbury to London as soon as possible was never carried out; the plan for the sees dependent on Canterbury achieved only partial fulfilment in 150 years, and little headway was made in the province of York. The kings of the Heptarchy lived most of their time in royal villages and the Church tended to follow the same pattern. Many of the bishops' seats were in small places and only in Canterbury, Rochester, London, Winchester, Leicester and York were they associated with the old Roman town pattern.

At present the archaeological evidence for any clearly recognisable organised life in London in the 5th and 6th centuries is almost entirely wanting. The city was a creation of its geographical position in relation to trade with the Continent in early Roman times. It rapidly grew into an important commercial centre and the focal point of the Roman road system. With the end of the Provinces and the occupation of the neighbouring lands by Anglo-Saxons it seems certain that most of the pre-requisites for London's existence came to an end for a while. Its political importance ceased catastrophically and any trading life between 450 and 550 must have been entirely local. Certain earthworks which ring round the London basin in Kent, Middlesex and the Chilterns have been invoked as evidence for the survival of a *"territorium"* of London, but the most important of these, Grim's Ditch in Middlesex, has now been shown to belong more probably to the Iron Age. A few of London's Romano-British inhabitants may have lingered on, but they are unlikely to have had much to do with the revival of the site which was later a matter of economic necessity.

By 604 London had been the chief place in the kingdom of Essex for some time and so received a bishop after the conversion. The stubborn heathenism of the Essex region and the importance of the patronage of the kings of Kent in the early days led the primacy to be seated at Canterbury, a fact of great importance in keeping London free from any powerful ecclesiastical control in the coming centuries. A hint of London's progress is provided by coins from a London mint found in the Crondall hoard dated to 610 - 630.

Although there are no details we know that London's revival was well under way in the late 7th and early 8th centuries when Bede could refer to the place as *multorum emporium populorum terra marique venientium* (the mart of many nations resorting to it by sea and land). Here, as elsewhere at this time, much of the early seaborne trade seems to have been in the hands of Frisian merchants.

Since 1945 important progress has been made in our knowledge of later Saxon towns at places like Thetford, Southampton, Canterbury, Ipswich, Oxford and Wareham. Nothing has yet been found which justifies the belief in any large developments before the 9th century, but the possibility of important discoveries which may show more traces of quasi-urban life in the earlier part of the period cannot be discounted. The large programme of work now in progress at Winchester is a case in point.

ANGLO-SAXON VILLAGES AND OTHER SETTLEMENT SITES

During this period the main settlement pattern of the towns and villages of England was established in detail, the balance of which was not seriously altered before the coming of the Industrial Revolution, and the Anglo-Saxon achievement in this respect is summarised in the Domesday Survey of 1086.

On the first edition of this map eighteen sites appeared on which there was clear evidence of settled life in the form of hut sites, domestic refuse, etc., plainly belonging to this period. Archaeology has not yet told us much about the characteristics of the early Anglo-Saxon village on this side of the North Sea. Some of the sites known may reasonably be regarded as those of nucleated villages, but so far none have any pretensions to size. Here and there isolated huts or small groups have been found as in some parts of the South Wolds of Lincolnshire and these cannot even be rated as hamlets.

The total number of known sites has now been raised past fifty and continues to increase. There are indications that we may now be approaching a break-through in this field, but we still have little enough for a period covering five hundred years. In the past the lack of sites has been partly due to an inability to recognise the domestic pottery of the pagan period and the wares which succeeded them in the 7th, 8th, and 9th centuries. Knowledge of Anglo-Saxon pottery is now increasing rapidly, thus removing a major bar to progress, but any detailed knowledge of the earlier communities is still wanting. Clearly a lot of the evidence for the early settlements must lie at the bottom of the stratification under modern communities which are their descendants. Such information as we have about the early groups at Sutton Courtenay in Berkshire and Wykeham in Yorkshire are due to their early destruction and the abandonment of the sites. It is unfortunate that for various reasons it was not possible to make a full examination of either, but a newly-discovered site like that at Puddlehill near Dunstable gives new opportunity. Here fair-sized huts with sunken floors are being found on a chalk site.

The meanness and squalor of these and other sites is remarkable and most of the structures found can have been no more than the homes of churls and serfs of low degree and work sheds. In the Anglo-Saxon homelands in the Low Countries and North-west Germany such miserable dwellings are common enough, but they are usually attendant on the large bow-sided, timber-built farmhouses of freemen which, on the evidence of German sites like Warendorf, were impressive structures as much as one hundred feet long and twenty-five feet wide. Until 1960 no comparable buildings belonging to this period had been found in a rural context in England. The first hint of a new development came in Maxey in Northamptonshire where traces of several rectangular buildings averaging fifty feet long and twenty feet wide have been found. These are not strictly comparable to the Warendorf type and finds made with them suggest a Scandinavian origin and a date in the 10th century. But the earliest phase of the Wessex royal manor at Cheddar has yielded a nearer approximation to it which is certainly Saxon and dates to the 8th century. Road work at Brampton in Huntingdonshire in 1961 has revealed a bow-sided building of Warendorf dimensions dated to the 10th century and now that a beginning has been made more will probably be recognised. The cutting of trenches across the sites of such buildings is liable to show little to the inexperienced eye because the wooden walls of these structures leave little obvious trace in ordinary soils. Today the increasing use of earth-moving machinery, although it can be very destructive of archaeological evidence, can sometimes reveal much of the entire plan of a structure at one stroke when earth is being graded off to a common level. Success here will depend on the presence of an experienced observer able to make a quick intervention.

No particular progress has been made in establishing a link between the Anglo-Saxon village and its burying ground. The impression given by the present evidence is that pagan cemeteries lay well away from the abode of the living towards the limits of the land held by the community. Later, with the coming of Christianity, preaching crosses with their enclosures were set up nearer the villages and become the site of the parish church. The dead were now buried in the shadow of the cross while their pagan forebears stayed on the confines to get occasional notice in boundary charters as "heathen burials".

ROYAL RESIDENCES AND *VILLAE REGALES*

In 1939 very little was known about the *villae regales* or royal residences of kings in the Dark Ages. From various sources, and chiefly from Bede, the general siting of a number of these was known, but none had ever been positively identified and studied. The poem "Beowulf" gives a glowing picture of the glories of Heorot, the hall of Hrothgar the Dane, but we have had to wait till 1955 to get any solid archaeological confirmation for this kind of place in Britain. This results from the discovery of two *villae regales* in Northumberland, Edwin's residence at Yeavering (Gefrin) and Oswald's close by at Milfield (Melmin). Both of these sites stand today on open agricultural land between Wooler and Berwick and were discovered by air-photography.

The excavation of the Yeavering site by Mr. Brian Hope-Taylor has revealed a remarkable complex of timber hall structures standing close to a stockaded defensive work. Two of the buildings are claimed to be a pagan shrine and a Christian church and it will be recalled that Paulinus baptised many of the Northumbrians in the adjacent river Glen in 627. The structures only survive in plan for all were built of wood.

One unexpected discovery appears to be another item in the debt of Northumbrian culture to the departed Roman world. This was a timber structure built for assemblies. In form it is an isolated *cuneus* of a timber amphitheatre—rather less than a quarter segment. At the focal point of this structure indications of a platform or throne site were found with other details suggesting the public uses to which it was put. The whole complex was comparatively short-lived and was destroyed by fire at least once, possibly by Cadwallon after his victory at Hatfield Chase in 632.

The Milfield site has not yet been excavated, but its numerous visible analogies with Yeavering along with the virtually certain identification of Milfield with the place name Melmin given by Bede to Oswald's seat put its character beyond doubt.

Another royal seat of this kind belonging to the kings of Wessex has now been examined at Cheddar in Somerset. This had a much longer life than the two Northumbrian examples because it was taken over as a going concern by the Norman kings after 1066 and after John's reign was in the hands of the Bishops of Bath and Wells till the Reformation. The earliest recognisable feature of the site was a long farmhouse-like structure with a general resemblance to the Warendorf type. There was also a storm water drain which limited the site on the north-west and contained stratified dating material. This early phase belonged to the 8th century. By the time of Alfred or somewhat later the main feature of the site was a large timber hall with an adjacent chapel, more than once reconstructed, and other buildings which have been interpreted as a bower, corn store, bakehouse and a mill worked by animal or slave power.

The finding of the royal ship burial at Sutton Hoo has focussed attention on Bede's statement that there was a royal residence of the East Anglian kings at Rendlesham nearby, but although a careful study of all the evidence by Dr. R.L.S. Bruce-Mitford has narrowed the area in which this residence must have stood, nothing definite is known of its precise site or details.

While kings spent much time in these *villae regales* during the period, we cannot doubt that their residences in places like Winchester, York, Canterbury, and Tamworth must have been of greater consequence. Some of these may have been no more than large royal "kraals", but the work now going on at Winchester may soon yield more positive information.

In Scotland and Wales information about royal sites is meagre. The Brittonic kingdom of Strathclyde had its principal fortress at Dumbarton and the kingdom of the Scots centred at Dunadd, but these places may not have contained important residences. The examination of Dunadd has given no information on this point and the prospects at the Rock of Dumbarton are hardly any better. St. Columba went to convert the Pictish king Brude mac Maelchon at a seat near Inverness (*munitio Brudei*) but of this there are no details. The scenes shown on the Pictish crosses suggest that Pictish rulers kept up a fair state if only because there was a high degree of craftmanship in the land. Other evidence is wanting.

In South Wales the home of a Welsh nobleman belonging to the period 500 - 700 has recently been examined at Dinas Powys near Cardiff. This was contained in a small re-adapted Iron Age promontory fort and its buildings had little pretension, but the finds made showed craft activities and wide contacts with the Mediterranean and Western European worlds beyond our expectations.

Finally in another section of the Celtic lands Castle Dore (Lancien), the residence of King Cunomorus or Mark of the Tristan and Isolde story near Fowey in Cornwall, was excavated in 1936-37. Here a deserted Iron Age hill fort had been taken over. The recognisable buildings consisted of two rectangular aisled timber halls measuring ninety feet by forty feet and sixty-five feet by forty-five feet with other structures which may have been kitchens and granaries. The entrance was also provided with two porter's lodges.

ANGLO-SAXON DEFENSIVE STRUCTURES

Little is yet known about Anglo-Saxon works defending enclosed areas before the time of King Alfred. There is no evidence of any attempt to adapt or use Roman defence works before the repair of the walls of London and Colchester in 886 and 891 by Alfred and Edward the Elder which is recorded in the Anglo-Saxon Chronicle. The use of the Saxon Shore forts at Burgh Castle, Bradwell-on-Sea and Reculver to house early monastic communities suggests that little interest was taken in their defensive possibilities except to use them as the *vallum monasterii* of these new foundations.

On the other hand the conditions under which some of the newcomers made their early settlements must have required bases with permanent defences. The rise of Bernicia which began in the later 6th century through a fiercely contested expansion inland from the coastal rock of Bamburgh must have required some fortification of that post. Nennius records that sometime between 575 and 600 the Bernicians were temporarily driven back into Holy Island by Urien of Rheged. We may also recall Bede's account of Penda's attack on Bamburgh during the harrying of Northumbria in 651 when Deira had temporarily become a province of Mercia. Unable to make any progress by siege or direct assault he tried to destroy the landward defences by burning the house materials of the neighbouring villages against them.

Nothing has yet been recognised of the Bernician defences of Bamburgh, but there is a fortified site close to the royal residence at Yeavering some sixteen miles inland which might be Anglo-Saxon. It occupies a nearly level sub-rectangular area about 500 feet across overlooking a steep slope down to the river Glen. This was surrounded by two timber stockades about 40 feet apart with large circular developments like guardhouses uniting the two on each side of the entrance. Enough work has been done on this to show that it is essentially native in origin and belongs to the class of double stockaded sites of the Roman Iron Age best exemplified in Southern Scotland at Harehope. While it may have been modified by Northumbrians it cannot be regarded as typical Anglo-Saxon work; it is just another example of the survival of a strong native element in this part of Northumbria.

There is little more to remark within the period except the earliest phase of the defences of Wareham in Dorset. These are partly secured by the parallel courses of the rivers Piddle and Frome on the north and south which have been completed by powerful banks and ditches to enclose a large rectangular area. The interpretation of these is in some dispute, but they are certainly post-Roman and may be the work of Egbert, the grandfather of Alfred. The case of Wareham raises the question of how many other places in Wessex were fortified in one way and another at the beginning of the 9th century. The Burghal Hidage of Edward the Elder's time gives details of a planned scheme of defence for Wessex which was inaugurated by Alfred and provided for the fortification and main-tenance of a large number of places. Some of these were Roman towns in which the original walls must have been surviving in some measure; it would seem improbable, however, that none of the others had possessed any defences before Alfred's time. In showing very few fortified Anglo-Saxon sites on this map we are not denying the possibility of many existing before 871 in all parts of England, but we do not know anything about them yet.

LINEAR EARTHWORKS

The most impressive monuments of the Dark Ages in Britain are the great linear earthworks which define boundaries and mark stages of conflict between Celts and Anglo-Saxons as well as episodes in the internecine wars of the Kings of the Heptarchy.

The scale and length of many of these works make any kind of continuous manning impossible. In a case like that of the Devil's Dyke on Newmarket Heath its size is such that it formed an obstacle not easily surmounted, but this is abnormal. They are often sited to cover important routes from one region to another and are usually to be regarded as emphatic definitions of boundaries rather than as purely military works.

Certain limited areas and periods excepted, linear earthworks first appear as a regular feature of prehistoric Britain in the Iron Age. Some defend the approaches to Belgic capital places and others, like the large series on the uplands of East and North Yorkshire, may have been connected with cattle-ranching, but otherwise they are slight and have the character of estate boundaries.

Two great linear defences, Hadrian's Wall and the Antonine Wall in Scotland, were of prime importance in the affairs of Roman Britain. Although they completely lost any importance about 450 they were an exemplar for both sides in the struggle between Briton and Anglo-Saxon and the Teutonic peoples also knew about Roman linear defences on the Continent long before they entered Britain.

In some cases the Dark Age date of linear earthworks is in no doubt where they are firmly associated with historical personalities and events, or have been shown to belong to this period by excavation. Others are less certain, but where their general character and tactical design suggest a Dark Age date they have been shown on the map.

There has recently been a revival of interest in the major Dark Age linear earthworks of the Wessex area. So far nothing has come to light to modify the interpretation of the Bokerly Dyke as a Romano-British ranch boundary later greatly strengthened and developed to resist West Saxon expansion into Dorset and the South-west. But the recent reconsideration of Wansdyke by Sir Cyril and Lady Fox has shown that this work has no real continuity over the forty-five miles between Dundry Hill, south-east of Bristol, and Great Bedwyn or thereabouts on the Berkshire-Wiltshire boundary. It is now seen to be two separate works, one cresting the hills south of the valley of the Bristol Avon between Bristol and Bath, and the other beginning at Morgan's Hill near Devizes and running along the summit of the Marlborough Downs to a point west of Savernake. The intervening section between the Avon east of Bath and Morgan's Hill is now known to be illusory and no more than the line of the Roman road from Silchester to Bath. Thus Wansdyke falls into two sections, a relatively slight western work and a much more imposing obstacle on the Marlborough Downs. Sir Cyril Fox attributes the eastern work to Ceawlin's desire to define and cover the northern limit of Wessex against the Angles of the Midlands after the battle of Fethanleag in 584. The western work may be the work of Romano-Britons covering their frontier against Ceawlin's expansion of Wessex to the Severn after his victory at Deorham in 577, but the more likely explanation is a Saxon defence of this part of the Wessex frontier against the growth of the Mercian kingdom under Penda *circa* 628.

Other works, like the Roman Rig and Becca Banks in Yorkshire may be similar coverage of the British kingdom of Elmet against Anglian expansion northwards from the Midlands. The most extensive of all linear earthworks in Britain are to be found between the Dee and the Bristol Channel where Wat's Dyke and Offa's Dyke represent two stages in the definition of the lengthy boundary between Mercia and the Welsh lands, and show the organising ability of a great Anglo-Saxon king at its highest.

The four dykes which span the open stretch of country between the East Anglian Heights and the Fenland in the neighbourhood of Royston, Cambridge and Newmarket have been the subject of some controversy. Archaeological evidence suggests that they are all post-Roman in date. It has been asserted that they are relics of a fluctuating frontier between Mercia and East Anglia, but the known facts of 7th century history do not support this. They may be the relic of a post-Mons Badonicus 6th century phase in which Anglo-Saxons in temporary retreat secured themselves in East Anglia against British pressure. However this may be they inspire considerable respect for the powers of their constructors. Less important, but perhaps belonging to the same early phase in East Anglian history, are the short lengths of dyke in West Norfolk.

The status of other dykes is less certain. The Chiltern Grim's Ditch has long been a crux, not only because of its failure to relate to any known Anglo-Saxon affairs, but also because of the oddities of its line across country which seem to make it little more than a set of local boundaries. An Iron Age date has recently been proposed for it, which seems to be more probable. There is also King Lud's Intrenchment sitting across the ancient Sewestern Lane line of communication between the South-east Midlands and the Trent Valley and now part of the boundary of Leicestershire.

Outlying systems of defensive works exist in general relation to a number of Roman towns like Colchester, St. Albans, Chichester, Cirencester and Silchester. In almost all cases there can be little doubt that these have reference to important centres of the late Iron Age which have preceded the growth of the Roman towns, and these works have all been omitted.

There remain a few other works like the Scot's Dyke in the Richmond area of Yorkshire, the Nico Ditch at Manchester, Comb's Ditch in Dorset, and the Giant's Hedge and Bolster Bank in Cornwall. None of these are of any strength, and the situation of those outside Cornwall suggests temporary frontiers of whose historical status we have no real knowledge.

In Scotland linear earthworks are mainly confined to the area between the Lammermuirs and the Cheviots. Of these the most important is the Catrail. The others are all short and generally take the form of cross-dykes barring old roads. None have been dated by excavation and no tradition connects them with historical events. In view of the disturbed history of much of the area until early modern times they cannot safely be placed in any period and are omitted from the map.

In Wales there are short dykes at various points along the Welsh side of Offa's Dyke, in Radnor Forest, and in the hill country overlooking the Vale of Glamorgan. Some of these are large enough to be shown on the map and are to be explained as forward works depending on Offa's Dyke. In general the South Welsh examples are very short, a quarter of a mile being an exceptional length, and their purpose is always to control movement along narrow ridgeways. Their age has never been proved, but all the attendant circumstances suggest a Dark Age origin. They have not been shown on the face of the map, but will be found in the accompanying lists.

An exception is the Clawdd Mawr in Carmarthenshire which is about half a mile long and covers the watershed between the rivers Teifi and Towy leading in the direction of the Mynydd Prescelly. This is considered to mark the boundary of the kingdom of Dyfed *circa* 720 and has been shown.

ANGLO-SAXON PAGAN BURIALS

Important finds which have been made since 1938 in other aspects of the field archaeology of the Anglo-Saxons have not deposed the individual burials and cemeteries of the period from their pre-eminence as the leading surviving traces of the early phases of the settlement. But while the presence of burials is virtual proof of the former existence of some kind of settlement not far away, the distributional relationship between the burials as they are known to us and the original topographical details of the settlement is far from clear. The incomers were farmers and we may expect the pattern of their life to be strongly governed by the occurrence of good land. In general this proves to be the case, but there is the corollary that the best land is liable to have been subjected to the most disturbance by centuries of cultivation with the probable destruction of a high proportion of the burials made in it. It is interesting to note that there are areas where many cemeteries might be expected, but they do not occur, while neighbouring marginal lands contain a fairly high number of burials. This is the case with the Trent valley from Nottingham to above Tamworth where we are concerned with the heartland of Mercia, but although there are early finds they are not numerous, and they contrast with the many surviving burials in the uplands of Derbyshire and Staffordshire close by. The explanation of this must be that the river lands have been much turned over while the marginal lands have escaped much disturbance of this kind until the building of enclosure walls and the barrow-digging craze of the 19th century.

Germane to this topic is the problem of the "heathen burials" which are sometimes mentioned as boundary features in the land charters of the Christian period. The sites of some of these can be securely identified on the ground, but neither ground inspection nor the use of air-photographs has so far revealed the traces of the barrows of a much earlier period which might have been used as landmarks and correctly attributed to heathen folk.

The possibility remains that these may be the traditional burial sites of the community before the Conversion. This question can only be settled by excavation and, if it should prove to be the case, it would appear that the dead were buried at the limits of their territory and well away from houses.

Sometimes burials were made in and round prehistoric barrows and there are also instances, such as the Snape boat burial, of an important grave being dug into and through other burials belonging to the Anglo-Saxons themselves. In some cases the occurrence of the humbler type of isolated warrior burial may reflect the casual incidents of fighting, but in the main the cemeteries must belong to settled groups. Pagan burials can occur over a period of at least three hundred years, though in the 7th century it is notorious that quite a large number of burials are probably Christian even though provided with grave goods. But, whatever the religious background of the burials, it can be said that the total number so far found and recorded either by cremation or by inhumation with grave goods is probably of the order of 20 - 25,000. This is a surprisingly modest figure for such a long time even when it is allowed that this can only be a small proportion (5%? 10%?) of all the burials made. Allowance must also be made for the short expectation of life in the period and the indifferent nature of the records. The largest cemeteries which have been examined with any approach to thoroughness seldom contain more than 800 to 1,000 burials. Most are far smaller, but often this may be due to partial destruction before examination or incomplete excavation. The smallness of the number remains impressive.

Within the inhumation cemeteries the graves often occur in distinct groups separately oriented and containing persons of all ages, both sexes and all conditions of life. These must be family groups. There is not much variation in the detail of the graves, but there are occasional abnormalities like burial on a bed. It seems that individual graves were sometimes marked by low mounds or by wooden posts or boards. Some graves on the chalk have sockets for such marks cut at the head and foot. Traces of small associated rectangular structures have been found among the burials at Lackford in Suffolk and at Alton in Hampshire. The former were considered to be Roman, but with no real certainty. Until more are found they must be obscure, but some sort of shrine or place of offerings may be involved. The possibility of these being found must be borne in mind in future excavations. There is also occasional evidence of some sort of fence round at least part of the cemetery and a few burials follow on as chance or deliberate appendages to already existing Romano-British burial places.

Many Anglo-Saxon burials occur as primary interments placed under barrows thrown up at the time, as opposed to secondary interments in older barrows of the kind frequent in Derbyshire and Wiltshire. Some of these primary barrow burials are well or even splendidly furnished as at Sutton Hoo, Taplow, Caenby and Benty Grange, but secondary interments can also vary from the lavishly equipped grave down to that with nothing but a small iron knife. Barrow burials, both primary and secondary, are most common in Kent, Sussex, Hampshire, Wiltshire and Derbyshire, but they occur sporadically in almost every area of early settlement. Perhaps the most anomalous inhumation cemeteries in England are those which have been made in the actual surfaces of Roman roads; in Watling Street over a distance of half a mile at Churchover near Rugby, and in the Fosse Way at Cotgrave near Nottingham.

It is difficult to give accurate expression to the different types of pagan Anglo-Saxon burial place on a map, and Dr. Crawford did not distinguish between cremation, inhumation and mixed cemeteries in the first edition. There was much to be said for his attitude and for the following reasons.

The rite used is no absolute criterion for the age of a pagan burial, but cremations must be relatively early although, in fact, the few Teutonic burials known in this country which antedate the end of the Roman province were by inhumation. These may belong to mercenaries and their dependents and do not appear on the map. Few pagan cemeteries have been completely excavated under modern conditions and still fewer have been adequately published. Some of the most famous like that in the King's Field at Faversham in Kent were destroyed in the course of construction work without being seen by any competent observer, and in this case the preservation of some of its riches was due to the enthusiasm of a local tradesman who bought many pieces from the workmen. We know nothing of how they were disposed in the graves. Further, it is never possible to be sure what the casual find of a single inhumation or cremation may imply unless further search is made in the area round about, and there must be finds shown on this map under the symbol for a small group which are the only present evidence for much larger assemblages. A warning instance of this is provided by the great cemetery at Sleaford in Lincolnshire. In the early 19th century burials were found which were dismissed as being those of persons who lost their lives in the Pilgrimage of Grace under Henry VIII. Later the Great Northern Railway was carried through the town and it chanced that Sleaford station was built close to the site of the earlier find. In due course a very large mixed Anglian cemetery was revealed containing at least 800 graves and occupying an area of some 3,600 square yards. But even where large cemeteries have been fully recognised other factors like piecemeal discovery over the years by desultory gravel digging may make the study of their original size and content difficult as at Mitcham in Surrey. A cemetery may contain only a few cremations compared with many inhumations or vice versa, but the uncertainty about the degree of exploration may make any attempt to classify it provisional. There is also the question of the religion of those buried. While it is fairly certain that most inhumations with grave goods will be those of pagans, such an assumption is not always correct. In the early days of the Conversion some of the Christian dead were buried in a style which is pagan to our eyes, though a study of all the circumstances will usually give a clue to the truth. It is not till the early 8th century that the older practice dies away. The most striking case of this lag is probably the Sutton Hoo ship burial which, though almost entirely pagan in content and apparent intention and also a cenotaph, probably commemorates a Christian king. In the latter part of our period Christian cemeteries can no longer be identified with any certainty. The occurrence of ancient burials away from churchyards and without any grave goods may belong to the period before churchyard burial became normal. The usual practice was to abandon the old pagan site and group the new burials round the crosses which were set up as local Christian centres. When in due course churches were built they often superseded the crosses on the same sites and so the earliest Christian dead became mingled with their successors. But occasional finds of pagan cremations and inhumations in village churchyards remind us that there can be continuity of site from pagan times to the present day.

The difficulties mentioned above may have weighed with Dr. Crawford, but an attempt has now been made to treat the various cemeteries as predominantly by cremation, or by inhumation, or as mixed; also to give effect to the different modes of barrow burial and to any other variants that there have been, having strict regard to the evidence which has come down to us. This has required the use of ten symbols. Mention must be made of a type of burial which is a newcomer since 1939. This is the ship or boat burial under a barrow. There are now three certain examples, all in East Anglia, two at Sutton Hoo and one at Snape, and both within a limited area of the coast of Suffolk. Although these are a striking addition to Anglo-Saxon archaeology it seems that they must be regarded as a local importation into East Anglia through the descent of the East Anglian royal house, the Uffings, from the kings of Uppland in Sweden where the custom of boat burial was normal among the aristocracy. They are therefore unlikely to be found outside the confines of the old East Anglian kingdom.

There are no great differences in pattern between the distributions which appeared in the first edition and those now set forth. It is chiefly a question of the further multiplication of sites which arises from another twenty-five years' work. On the northern and western fringes of the Anglo-Saxon area there has been some modest increase, but this does not extend to that part of Northumbria north of the Tyne. Here, in spite of the early rise of the Anglian kingdom of Bernicia, there is none of that evidence of early settlement which is provided by pagan cemeteries. Howick is a small and doubtful exception, but does little to cover the eighty years between Ida and Edwin. This could be due to a much earlier spread of Christian influence from the north than we know of. One is left with the impression that Bernicia consisted of a small Anglian aristocracy ruling a largely native population.

Equally the pagan burials of Wessex still do not encroach beyond the western limits of Salisbury Plain and there is still very little in East Dorset. On the outer limits of the Anglo-Saxon world in the early 7th century we are entitled to wonder if the possession of no more than a spear and a knife must always be the mark of an Anglo-Saxon burial.

Over the map as a whole the symbol showing the burial of from one to three individuals has multiplied in most places. Often it is quite likely that no more than an outlying warrior burial is concerned, but sometimes we may expect new finds to raise the status of these lone burials to that of cemeteries in the next edition.

ANGLO-SAXON SHRINES AND HOLY PLACES

Knowledge of these is still slight and almost wholly non-archaeological. It mainly derives from the evidence of place names which recall the former existence of shrines and from statements in the literature of the time.

There is Bede's story about the conversion of Edwin of Northumbria when Coifi, the chief priest of the old religion, took the leading part in the destruction of the pagan shrine at Goodmanham in the East Riding of Yorkshire. The compromise of Redwald, king of the East Angles, who thought he could avoid political difficulties arising from his own conversion by setting up an altar to Christ side by side with those of the old pagan gods also comes to mind. But the only archaeological evidence of a pagan shrine comes from the royal manor of Yeavering where one of the rectangular timber buildings has been interpreted as such. This confirms the various hints that these holy places were covered buildings and from other sources we may be sure that they contained wooden idols and had enclosures round them. The great example is the building with mighty wooden pillars which once stood on the site of the present cathedral at Uppsala. Similar evidence may lie under some of our own churches for Gregory the Great consented to the taking-over of heathen shrines by Christians provided that they were purified and the idols removed.

The principal elements in place names which may be associated with the old religion are the names of the gods Thunor and Woden, the word *hearg* meaning a sacred grove or heathen temple, and the word *weo* or *wig* meaning an idol. Examples of these are Thunderfield, Thundersley, Wednesbury, Wenslow, Harow on the Hill, Peper Harrow, Weyhill and Weoley. Names of features like Harrowdown Hill are also significant.

MONASTERIES

Monasteries as such did not appear on the south sheet of the first edition, though some of the principal places concerned received a church symbol. On the north sheet eight cashels were shown, all among the western islands.

An attempt has now been made to show all known monastic sites. The part played by monasteries in evangelising Britain both from Ireland and from the Continent is well known. In our period the monasteries of the Celtic and Saxon churches were similar in their organisation. The formal plan, which was a regular feature of the monastic house in the full Middle Ages, did not enter England before the reforms of the 10th century associated with Cluny.

The common feature of all early monastic establishments in Britain was the enclosure or *vallum monasterii* surrounding the buildings which were themselves set out on no regularly observed plan. Sometimes early monasteries were established in sites with pre-existing defences like native or Roman forts, good examples being St. Fursey's house in Burgh Castle (Gariannonum-Cnobheresburg), St. Cedd's at Bradwell-on-Sea (Othona-Ythanceaster), St. Cybi's in the little Roman fort at Holyhead, and possibly Dundarg in Scotland. Excavation has now revealed the large bank and ditch which surrounded the early monastic precinct at Glastonbury. Sometimes the barrier was no more than a hedge or turf wall, and in Scotland the cashels were normally of dry stone construction.

A single symbol has therefore been used to show all monastic establishments known to have existed before 871. In some cases their precise location is not known although we can place them within a mile of the spot, and our only evidence comes from the lives of the saints which show that they were educated at, or went out from, monasteries at named places about which we should otherwise be ignorant.

At this time monasteries were normally quite independent of each other and there was nothing which could be compared with the Europe-wide organisation of the later monastic orders, but since some major houses like Medeshamstede (Peterborough) sent out groups of monks to found colonies at other places, there were several examples of federations of houses sprung from the same source. In this the influence of notable founders like St. Aldhelm and St. Wilfrid was paramount, and the latter was responsible for introducing the Benedictine rule which was observed in many Saxon monasteries.

The form which the organisation of an early monastic house took depended on the ideas of the founder. Thus double monasteries for men and women were not uncommon, and women, as abbesses, had great influence and authority which sprang from their rank as well as from their personal qualities. Princesses of the Anglo-Saxon royal houses were prominent in early monastic life, and the whole of English history before the Reformation can hardly show a more powerful female personality than St. Hild of Whitby. It was not infrequent for a whole family to resolve to devote itself to the religious life, take vows, build a church, and receive confirmation for their new house from kings and bishops.

But monasticism was in serious danger of extinction at the close of our period. The multiplication of small houses *(monasteriola)* of the family type was sometimes dictated not by genuine religious zeal but by a wish to avoid the payment of various public obligations. It reached such a pitch that the foundations of the state were endangered at a critical time. There was also considerable laxity in the more important houses and all these evils are clearly set out in Bede's letter to Bishop Egbert of York in 734. A system already suffering from internal decay was exposed to the ferocious attack of the Northmen during the 9th century and collapsed. Famous houses were destroyed and their inmates murdered or scattered; Dom David Knowles has given it as his opinion that in 871 no monastic house is likely to have survived north and east of Watling Street while in the south and west the Rule of St. Benedict had probably been abandoned except at St. Augustine's, Canterbury.

Monastic life was not to revive until the victories of the House of Wessex and the labours of Dunstan and Ethelwold put it on a new footing by introducing the reforming spirit of Cluny in the 10th century.

BISHOPRICS

Anglo-Saxon bishoprics were established upon a territorial basis. A bishop had authority over a region, generally the territory of a particular people, or group of kindred peoples, and placed his seat at some convenient point within it. These seats are shown on the map by a bishop's mitre; it will be noted that they were sometimes places of little importance then or now. Where Roman town sites were used some recognition of their former status was given by the use of the term *civitas* in describing them.

Celtic bishoprics were in no sense territorial and so cannot generally be given a location on the map, but a limited number of sites strongly associated with early bishops and which later became established as bishops' seats have been shown. For the difference between Celtic and Saxon bishoprics see Dom Gougaud, *Christianity in Celtic Lands*, English translation, 1932, 216 - 220.

SECULAR CHURCHES

The identification and dating of early churches in Britain has made much progress in recent years. Many of the more famous examples have been critically re-examined and in humbler buildings important early features have been recognised for the first time. Besides this there has been much re-assessment of the many fragments of early sculpture which have been found in churchyards or have survived built into churches. The total body of material is now formidable and is too large to be shown on a map of 1:1,000,000 scale which has to carry much other material. Thus only the fully established examples of secular churches earlier than 871 are shown and the inclusion of some of these may be controversial.

The parish church as understood today was a thing of modest growth before 871. Evidence relating to it is bound to be slight after more than a thousand years and the humble church in an obscure place has more chance of coming through to us than more important buildings. Excavation has shown that churches were built on royal estates as at Yeavering and Cheddar. It is probable that noblemen followed suit on their own lands, but the provision of a church in every village was still far distant. Most of the churches built in this period were those of monastic communities and were known as minsters. Local religious needs were met by the creation of consecrated places or enclosures *(loci)* where services could be held and the dead buried, and these were served by priests who came from the minsters. St. Willibald's dedication to the religious life took place at the foot of the cross at one of these places. His "Life", composed in the 8th century, says: "for it is the custom of the Saxon people to erect on the estates of nobles, not a church, but the standard of the Holy Cross, set up on high for the frequency of daily prayer". These *loci* were fenced in and provided with a cross of wood or stone. It is a fair presumption that later they often became the sites of parish churches and by a fortunate chance an apparent instance of this continuity has recently been found at Stafford. The site of the medieval church of St. Bertolin has been excavated and two churches have been found beneath it, the earlier a small wooden structure and the later a stone church of the 11th century. A surprising find was a massive wooden cross buried beneath the floor of the wooden church which may be the original cross of the *locus* preserved from base uses by being buried under the church which succeeded it.

Seventeen churches belonging to this period were shown on the first edition in addition to those at Hexham, Ripon, Rochester and Canterbury which were then classed under cathedrals. Now that monasteries are being treated separately most of the former list of churches has been absorbed into this category.

CHAPELS AND HERMITAGES

The life of the early Celtic Church gave rise to minor Christian monuments and sites which cannot conveniently be placed in the categories of monasteries and churches. These are principally hermitages and chapels. Details of plan and remoteness of situation will usually help to distinguish between ordinary monasteries and the abodes of anchorites, both male and female, who sometimes exercised considerable influence on Church affairs. Examples are the remains on the outlying island of North Rona and on the islets of St. Helen's and Tean in the Scillies at opposite ends of the British world. Ynys Seiriol (Puffin Island) off the coast of Anglesey is a case where the surviving plan of the earliest phase fully supports its interpretation as a hermitage.

St. Ninian's Cave near Whithorn is an example of a natural feature used as an oratory and there are also the enigmatic sites which may be associated with him at Brampton and Brougham in Cumbria which lay in the ancient kingdom of Rheged. Most obvious and numerous are the clear cases of early chapels. The greatest surviving assemblage is in the Isle of Man. Christianity was already established here by the end of the 5th century and at this stage the island fell within the sphere of influence of Wales rather than Ireland. The ancient land division was the small unit known as the 'treen'. Each of these had its own Christian centre which began as a 'rhullick' (from the Latin *reliquiae*), a burial place of round or oval plan enclosed by a bank. These were originally marked by simple standing crosses and the dead were buried there in the characteristic 'lintel' (long cist) graves. They were also places for the celebration of Christian rites and in due course small chapels known as 'keeills' were set in them. The dating of these is not always certain because they kept a primitive form through the succeeding Norse period and on into modern times, but the number whose pre-871 date is certain is considerable. Other examples of this kind outside Man may be seen at St. Ninian's in Bute, at Chapel Finnian near Whithorn and near St. David's in West Wales.

MEMORIAL STONES

These are inscribed pillar stones, for the most part unworked, which were placed to mark the graves of the dead in the Celtic parts of Britain in the 5th, 6th, and early 7th centuries. The inscriptions on them are normally in Latin in late Roman script, but sometimes they are doubled on the same monument by an Irish version in the Ogam script, and occasionally Ogams alone appear. In general the form of the inscription or the presence of a Christian symbol puts it beyond doubt that the person commemorated was a Christian, but this cannot be assumed in every case. Many of them have been found in churchyards or built into later churches. Others stand in lonely situations among the hills, sometimes close to old trackways.

Nothing analogous to the memorial stone has come to us from Roman Britain although the existence of Christianity among the population is in no doubt. This form of monument is first met with in Ireland before the 5th century and its appearance in Western Britain must probably originate with the movement of Irish people into Wales and Cornwall. The formula of the Latin inscriptions used on these stones is that used in contemporary Christian Gaul and the vertical application of the

Ogams to the edges of the stones is typically Irish. We thus have evidence of two extraneous influences at work, one certainly due to the connections between the Irish Sea area and Western France which is strongly borne out in the accounts of the travels of the Celtic saints. Many of the West Britons had emigrated to Britanny and the Loire valley and contacts between Britons on both sides of the western part of the Channel were frequent.

Memorial stones occur in considerable numbers in Wales and Cornwall and to a lesser extent in Devon, the Isle of Man and the region between the Tyne and the Forth. The relative densities of their distribution may be taken as some evidence of the degree of survival of a feeble Romanity in the Celtic areas of the West and North. In Scotland they may be a product of the mission of St. Ninian between 397 and 432, but in any area some of them may antedate the end of the Roman province. In only two cases is there direct internal evidence of dating; from the Penmachno stone (C.I.I.C. No. 396; Nash Williams, No. 104) where the consulate of Justinus mentioned belongs to 540, and Llangadwaladr (Nash Williams, No. 13) where the King Cadfan commemorated died *circa* 625.

In Wales the stones form two groups in North and South Wales respectively, divided by a wide belt of empty country in the centre. In South Wales there is a heavy concentration in Pembroke-shire with lesser numbers in Carmarthenshire, Breconshire and Glamorgan. In North Wales the numbers are less, but evenly distributed over the whole area north of a line joining the Mawddach estuary to the upper course of the Dee. The distribution in South-west England covers the whole of the peninsula west of Dartmoor with a group in the South Hams of Devon and outliers on Exmoor. There is also an extreme outlier, Ogam-inscribed and enigmatic in its isolation, at Silchester in Hampshire.

It is in Wales and the South-west that the Ogam inscriptions predominate, with a major concentration in West Wales. They and the personal names recorded on them are evidence for a considerable degree of Irish settlement in these regions which took place chiefly in the late 4th century, possibly as *foederati* to protect these areas against their own freebooting kin. The smaller number of Ogams in North Wales may be due to the early subjugation of the Irish settlers by other federates transferred from the Lothian area under Cunedda in the late 4th or early 5th centuries, an interruption which did not occur in South Wales or in Devon and Cornwall until the conquest of the latter area by the Kings of Wessex between 700 and 850. In a number of cases there is evidence that Ogam inscriptions were deliberately defaced on some of the stones. Uncertain traces of the ends of Ogam scores sometimes survive and make it difficult to reckon the precise number of these inscriptions.

In the North the distribution of memorial stones is sporadic in the Lowlands of Scotland. Irish Ogams are absent from all but two in Southern Argyll, but these may be the result of the Scotic movement into that area. An interesting feature is the association of two Latin-inscribed stones with long cist cemeteries, the Catstane at Kirkliston in Midlothian and the Yarrow Stone in Selkirkshire. There are also a few of particular interest in the far North in which the language used is Pictish.

The chief authorities for these stones are the *Corpus Inscriptionum Insularum Celticarum* of R.S. Macalister, V.E. Nash Williams' *Early Christian Monuments of Wales* (Cardiff, 1950), and H.O'N. Hencken's *Archaeology of Cornwall and Scilly*, (Methuen's County Archaeologies, 1932).

The continued independence of Wales and the uninterrupted Christian life in the area gave rise to a large number of monuments, mostly funerary in the form of crosses, which span the rest of the period. The memorial stones of the earlier phase and the later monuments have been distinguished as two classes on the map. In general all those occurring outside Wales may be regarded as belonging to the earlier class and in Devon and Cornwall there appears to be little which can be safely dated later than 700.

LONG CIST AND SUB-ROMAN CEMETERIES

The Celtic world outside the areas of early Anglo-Saxon domination has produced a variety of cemeteries and burials, presumably Christian in most cases, which have been recognised in Scotland, Wales and the West of England, and may also be expected in the western parts of Northern England.

The most notable group of these is found in Southern Scotland. They are called long cist cemeteries because the dead are inhumed without any grave goods in coffin-like arrangements of larger or smaller stones. Cist burials are no prerogative of any one period; most undoubtedly prehistoric burials of this type are in short cists and contain either a crouched inhumation or a cremation.

They show a tendency to megalithic construction when the material for it is available.

Long cist burials predominate in the Lothian region of Scotland. Here is a concentration of cemeteries varying in size from several hundred graves to groups of three or four burials. On the south its distribution is bounded by the Lammermoors and only one or two examples have been found in the valleys draining southwards into the Tweed. Northwards the type crosses the Forth and is found round the coasts of Fife and Angus as far north as the borders of Kincardineshire with few examples sited very far inland. In two cases, at Kirkliston in Midlothian and at Yarrow in Selkirkshire, they have been found in general association with memorial stones which are presumably Christian and not later than 6th century in date.

The burials are normally oriented with the head to the west and no grave goods have been found with any of them. While there is no formal proof it is difficult to doubt that these burials are Christian. Their area shows some agreement with that covered by the Northumbrian advance to the Forth and beyond till 685, but too much stress must not be laid on this. Burials of this kind have not yet been found in the Northumbrian homeland.

Long cist burials occur in other parts of Scotland far from the Lothians. Graves at Galson in Lewis, Kilmartin in Argyll and Terally in Wigtownshire may be cited, but the only other area in which there is a comparable concentration is the Isle of Man. Here the early Christian sites known as rhullicks and keeills produce many "lintel" graves which may be equated with the long-cist type. Similar graves at Clynnog-fawr and Trearddur Bay in North Wales are certainly associated with Christian sites.

Turning to Southern Britain we find that although large western and northern areas remained free from Anglo-Saxon conquest for at least two hundred years after the collapse of the Roman provinces it is surprising that very few groups of burials have been clearly recognised as likely to belong to this time. In Wales, Cornwall and Devon memorial stones survive which imply Christian burials, but there has been little directly established association between these and human remains.

The examination of the large cemetery at Cannington Park by the estuary of the Parrett in Somerset has shown that it was in use from the 4th to possibly the 8th century. It now becomes apparent that other groups of inhumations found in the Bristol Channel area must belong broadly to the same period. Several of them at Llantwit Major, Banwell, Yatton and Henbury have been placed in the ruins of Roman villas and must post-date their destruction by some time. The cemetery at Camerton by the Foss Way, while clearly Christian, has nothing in it to give it a decisively Saxon character. All these cemeteries have therefore been placed on the map in the general category of sub-Roman in the hope that this will lead to further discoveries.

PICTISH SYMBOL STONES AND CROSS SLABS

The only important examples of Pictish art which have survived are stone monuments. These divide into two principal classes, rough pillars or boulders bearing combinations of symbols and cross slabs of a distinctive type, sometimes elaborately carved which may also incorporate some of these symbols on their backs or in the frontal schemes of decoration. Pictish symbols have been found incised on the walls of caves at Covesea in Moray and at East Wemyss in Fife. There is also a small class of incised animal figures of which the group of six stones carved with the figures of bulls found at Burghead in Moray is the best known.

The distribution of the Pictish symbol stones proper covers the whole of the eastern part of Scotland north of the Forth as far as the Orkneys and Shetlands. They are found over most of the habitable part of this area. In the southern part of Pictland Fife has its quota, but the main concentration is in Strathmore and up the valleys of the Tay and Earn. There is a gap in Kincardineshire where the mountains come down to the sea, and the distribution is resumed in the valleys of the Dee and Don with a heavy concentration in the hinterland of Aberdeenshire. A gap follows till Speyside and Moray are reached when they are again plentiful. The most northerly group begins on Loch Ness, passes by Inverness, and extends through the coastal parts of Ross and Cromarty to form a final nucleation round Golspie in Sutherland. A few more tail out northwards along the coast of Caithness and into the Northern Islands. Elsewhere there are a few in the Western Islands, principally in Skye, and there are three outliers remote from Pictland proper at Dunadd in Argyll, Anwoth in Kirkcudbrightshire and Roberton near Hawick.

Symbol stones carry varying incised combinations of some seventeen different symbols whose meaning is unknown, though it has been suggested that they may have had a quasi-heraldic significance. The latest and best study of these stones has been made by R.B.K. Stevenson *The Problem of the Picts* (Nelson, 1955). He concludes that no artistic development can be ascribed to the Picts earlier than the mid-7th century on the present evidence, and that the main sources of their art are to be found in the Hiberno-Saxon styles from the 7th to the mid-8th centuries. The animal forms may have come from the Mediterranean art of the 6th and 7th centuries through the medium of Northumbria, though the genius of the Pictish artist made its own distinctive mark on them.

The purpose of symbol stones has long been uncertain, but the clear use of one to mark a triple grave at Birsay in Orkney and a probable association with graves at Easterton of Roseisle provides the clue. In any case few symbol stones are in their original positions when found.

When the Picts began to set up crosses in the middle of the 8th century they did not choose to follow the example of Northumbria and the Scots by adopting the free-standing cross. Instead they used dressed stone slabs, sometimes rectangular, and sometimes expanding in width towards the base. The Pictish sculptors took full advantage of the large field provided on front and back so that the decoration of these slabs is often elaborate. There are also other forms besides cross slabs such as the monumental slabs to be seen at Meigle and elsewhere.

These monuments range from the middle of the 8th century to the beginning of the 11th century by which time the Picts had lost their independence and their art, exposed to many outside influences, lost its identity.

The earliest of these cross slabs are found in the south of Angus and Perthshire, but by the beginning of the 9th century they begin to appear on the Moray Firth and in the Northern Islands. While they remain highly individual monuments to the last they embody various features borrowed from Northumbria, Ireland and late classical art like the inhabited vine scroll and boss decorations. Pictish symbols continue to appear on them until the mid-9th century after which their absence may be symptomatic of the loss of Pictish independence with the establishment of the United Kingdom under Kenneth mac Alpin. Outstanding features of these slabs are the vigorous hunting, battle and biblical scenes carved on them.

There is little doubt that the symbol stones as well as the cross slabs fall within the period of Christianity and the former view that the symbols represent a survival of La Tene art kept in Scotland through the Roman period is no longer tenable. The use of the symbols is in no way incompatible with Christianity.

Finally, symbols also occur on a few portable objects like hand pins, Pictish silver chains and pieces of bone.

OGAM INSCRIPTIONS IN SCOTLAND

The system of writing called Ogam was invented in Ireland and the spread of its use over Great Britain is a fair index of the extension of Irish or Hiberno-Scottish influence in our period. Under the heading "Memorial stones" its use for funerary inscriptions in Wales, Cornwall and Dalriadic Scotland has already been mentioned, and this has historical importance in showing areas where Irish settlement was considerable in the early Dark Ages. But in the absence of these inscriptions we should still have a good knowledge of the Irish language of the time from other sources. Some Ogam inscriptions are also found distributed over the Pictish area of Scotland with a strong local concentration in Shetland. Only twenty eight examples are known and they occur variously on memorial stones, Pictish symbol stones, cross slabs, stones of uncertain purpose and even, in two cases, on bone knife handles. Little is known about the languages spoken in Pictland during the Dark Ages and so this pitifully small body of epigraphy has an importance disproportionate to its size. The best opinion today is that some of the Picts, at least, spoke a P-Celtic Gallo-Brittonic tongue and the language used in some of these inscriptions is certainly Celtic, but in others as at Altyre, Inverurie, St. Madoes (Inchyra House) and Lunnasting some incomprehensible non-Indo-European language seems to be employed. The occurrence of so many of the "Pictish" Ogams in the far north is a tribute to the wide extension of Scotic influence. Their associations suggest that they belong to the 8th and 9th centuries, or even later. There are only one or two cases like the inscription on the Auquhollie stone which can possibly be as old as the 5th century. Both the "Irish" and the "Pictish" Ogams are indicated on the map.

FREE-STANDING CROSSES

Crosses of this type belonging to the early days of Christianity can be found in most parts of Great Britain. While it is probable that the earliest examples were set up in the South as a result of the Augustinian conversion, most of the finest survivors occur north of a line joining the mouth of the Severn to the Wash. Many were made of wood. Thus their survival is not to be expected, though one has been found buried under the chancel of a later church (St. Bertolin's, Stafford) and traces of many more probably lie in similar situations, placed there when superseded by the building of a church.

These early crosses indicated places where the Gospel was preached and where the local people gathered to hear the Mass celebrated by priests coming from minsters and to bury their dead under the protection of the sacred symbol. The rhullicks of the Isle of Man are examples of these places. At a later stage elaborately carved stone crosses continued to be set up near churches and elsewhere. Sometimes they commemorated a person as at Bewcastle and Hexham, and at Dewsbury a great cross was set up which recalled the ministry of Paulinus. In North Britain the conditions were broadly the same, but while crosses of Northumbrian and Irish inspiration were free-standing, all the earlier Pictish examples were carved on slabs some of which also carried combinations of Pictish symbols.

There has been much controversy about the dating and artistic affiliation of crosses. In many cases the finding of early cross fragments near a medieval church allows a strong presumption that an early church stood on the same site. The total number of fragments which can be regarded as older than the mid-9th century is considerable and cannot be given full treatment on a map of this scale. In North Britain an attempt has been made to show all Pictish, Scotic and Northumbrian crosses which fall in this period. In South Britain only the most famous crosses are shown. In most cases they are reasonably well preserved, but there are exceptions where the great interest of the surviving fragments secures their inclusion.

EVIDENCES OF SETTLED LIFE IN NORTH BRITAIN

This subject is bedevilled by the fact that while there are many undefended minor settlements of various kinds plain to be seen in all parts of North Britain, we have not yet solved the problem of how to distinguish those which belong to our period. Datable material is not often found (coins are absent) and though a structural sequence can sometimes be established it is difficult to relate its phases to centuries, let alone decades, of historical time.

Southern Pictland, chiefly concerned with the modern counties of Fife, Angus, Kincardine and Aberdeen, must always have been one of the most populous regions because of its natural advantages. It is here that we should be able to form some idea of the life of the Picts, in an area where many surviving sculptures attest an important settled population and numerous examples of earth-houses (souterrains) should give some clue to the settlement pattern. The work of the late F.T. Wainwright at Carlungie decisively confirmed the association of earth-houses with simple structures which were essentially farms, but here the only datable object was a brooch belonging to the Roman period. This could be a survival and it is reasonable to suppose that the daily life of the Southern Picts in the Dark Ages was related to sites of this kind, but unfortunately earth-houses are not in themselves indicative of any particular period, occurring at any time between the Late Bronze Age and the Middle Ages.

Further north we enter the country of the brochs, the defensive towers whose main period of occupation covers the first few centuries of our era. The siting of these is related to the better land, where continuous occupation is to be expected, but it is only at Jarlshof, at the southern tip of Shetland, that we can see clearly the progression from a broch to a small village, whose life certainly extended into the Dark Ages. This group consisted of some of the specialised northern dwellings known as wheel-houses along with field huts, and there was evidence of both agriculture and cattle-keeping. The inhabitants made a poor but distinctive pottery which may have diagnostic value for the north in the future. In due course this village was supplanted by intrusive Northmen. Other broch sites in the north, which have not been so thoroughly examined, have yielded evidence of similar post-broch occupation, but its duration is quite uncertain. Much the same might be said of individual wheel-houses, which are plentiful in the Western Islands. Some of these were occupied in Roman times and after they had fallen into ruin they harboured squatters, but we can only be reasonably sure of those secondary phases which belong to the Middle Ages. Finally on the mainland, and notably in

Sutherland, there are found numerous circular houses, usually in groups and often incorporating souterrains, though of a simpler type than those of Southern Pictland. An excavated example at Kinbrace yielded material similar to that from the secondary occupation of some broch sites, but since these structures appear to have continued well into the Middle Ages they do not form a class that can be included on this map.

Dalriada has virtually nothing to show and Strathclyde is little better. In the South-west sites exist but we cannot date them, and the trifling amount of imported Dark Age pottery from Buston crannog is all that dates any settlement site to this period. In Manau Guotodin and the area of Northumbrian extension to the Forth the numerous long cist cemeteries must have some relation to settlements but none have yet been recognised. In the Lowlands and passing through the Cheviot area into Northumberland we encounter the so-called "Scooped" sites which are believed to have had an occupation extending into the Dark Ages and later. These are usually placed along the line of low terrace overlooking the course of a stream. They were made by scooping out a large shallow excavation with an entrance towards the water. The limits of the compound thus formed were further defined by a certain amount of upcast material to which boulders were sometimes added. Inside the compound the sites of one or two round huts may be seen and there is sometimes evidence of later re-use of the site in the form of ruined secondary rectangular structures. These sites may be either solitary or strung in sequence along a terrace. Such little evidence as there is suggests a beginning in Roman times with later continuation. There are also enclosed hut groups in Northumberland where occupation in the post-Roman period is certain. These sites belong to a region extending from the Forth towards the Tyne which belonged to the Votadini in later Roman times.

Little more can usefully be said, but work on the different types of ancient rural settlement in North Britain is going on under the aegis of the Royal Commission on Ancient and Historical Monuments of Scotland through the production of county inventories which are preceded by a thorough examination of the ground.

FORTRESSES IN THE CELTIC LANDS

Scotland

Scotland had her fair share of fortresses of Iron Age type when Agricola began his attempt to conquer the country in the 1st century. These were for the most part hill-forts of dry-stone construction with internal timber bracing and many were destroyed by fire. It is unknown whether in any given case this was due to Roman slighting, inter-tribal warfare, or mere accident, but the product— a vitrified fort — was the same. For the next three centuries Roman policy and fortunes in Scotland fluctuated, but we may be sure that for the most part the regions north of the Forth-Clyde line suffered only occasional interference. The only site of the later Roman period about which much is known is the important centre at Traprain Law in East Lothian.

The opening of the period saw the establishment of a new pattern of power. The chief contenders were the newly-arrived Scots in Argyll, the Northern and Southern Picts, and the two Brittonic realms of Strathclyde and Manau Guotodin — the last destined to an early collapse. Two principal classes of fortresses now claim our attention. The first may be called "historic" because they play their part in the shadowy wars of the period and are specifically mentioned in the meagre annals of the time. They are Dunadd, Dunollie, Dumbarton, Dundurn, Dunbar, Dunnottar and Duneidin. Among them Dunadd and Dunollie were principal strongholds of the Scots, Dumbarton (Altclut) was the capital of the Strathclyde Britons and only Dundurn and Dunnottar fall in the Pictish area. Their general siting on steep crags, their dry-stone construction and the re-use of the sites in later times have combined to leave little or nothing of any Dark Age structures. Only Dunadd has yielded a few finds clearly showing Dark Age occupation.

These may be placed on the map without hesitation, but it is otherwise with the second class. Here we have a number of sites which show a more or less completely ruined fortress of Iron Age type containing a simple secondary ring-work with thick dry-stone wall enclosing a small area on the highest part of the site. Good examples of this occur at Turin Hill in Angus and at Dunearn in Fife. No archaeological proof has yet been forthcoming for the date of these ring-works. A case has also been argued for a class of "nuclear" forts of presumed Dark Age date in which a strong defence of the summit is supplemented by a number of lesser enclosures below, which take advantage of defensive features of the ground, but this has not gained acceptance. There can be little doubt that the defences of the secondary ring-work could be of Dark Age date but, pending more acceptable evidence on the whole question, this second edition can do little more than repeat the practice of the first in showing "historic" sites.

On a lower level there is the large class of minor forts collectively known as duns. These have a number of variations of plan, but no evidence has yet been forthcoming that any originate in the Dark Ages. They belong essentially to the Iron Age and are of the same period as the greater forts which suffered vitrification. Few have been thoroughly excavated and when any Dark Age material has been found it has always been in a secondary position concerned with some later squatting. Cases in point are Dun Cuier, Dun Scurrival and Dun Bhan, all on Barra, where material with a lower date early in the 7th century has been found. Further south in the fort at Ugadale Point in Kintyre there were signs of occupation as late as the 8th century and the galleried dun at Kildonan Bay in the same area seems to have been lived in from the 3rd to the 7th centuries. An interesting case is the Mote of Mark on the coast of Kirkcudbrightshire where an Iron Age timber-laced fort was destroyed by fire and then attracted another occupation in the Dark Ages which has left evidence in the form of pottery and clay moulds for making jewellery covering the period from the 5th to the 8th centuries. The defensive scheme of this second phase, if any, is not known. Sound grounds may be forthcoming for the appearance of nuclear and ring forts on the next edition, but meanwhile the treatment of this subject in Scotland must be confined to certainties.

WALES

At present there is no evidence that any serious attempt was made to re-establish the defences of the old Iron Age hill fort system after the close of the Roman period. Some major North Welsh forts were still in use in Roman times. Tre'r Ceiri defended a sizeable community and there was an at present inexplicable reconstruction of the defences of Dinorben in the 2nd century while the hill top of the Breidden was also inhabited in the 3rd and 4th centuries.

The occurrence of a very crude form of pottery on a number of Welsh sites has been claimed as evidence for post-Roman re-occupation. This pottery was first recognised in any quantity at the enclosed hut-group of Pant y Saer in Anglesey, but there is no reason to believe that the occupation of this place extended far into the 5th century and experience at Castell Odo, a hill fort in the Lleyn peninsula, has shown that here this kind of pottery belonged to an Iron Age occupation dated to several centuries before the Roman conquest. The same sort of material has been found at the Breidden, Garn Boduan, Old Oswestry, Eddisbury and, doubtfully, at Dinorben. All of these sites had an Iron Age origin which, in the absence of unambiguous stratigraphical evidence to the contrary, suggests that this pottery may belong to it and equate them with Castell Odo.

On the other hand there was certainly some Dark Age resort to some of them and excavation of the hill top at Dinas Emrys has borne out ancient traditions about the occupation of the site in this period. A small dry-stone fort containing a single round house at Carreg y Llam on the coast of Caernarvonshire seems to belong to the 5th century or later. A few scraps found at Deganwy (Arx Decantorum) also hint at Dark Age occupation, but no defences have been found.

All of these sites belong to North Wales. As a fully integrated part of the Roman province South Wales was in a different position, but it is here that work on a small Iron Age fort re-used by a Welsh chieftain at Dinas Powys outside Cardiff has given the clearest indications of pottery, glass and metal work which can be firmly placed between the 5th and 7th centuries. One of the four defensive banks on the site may be the work of this period, but the later building of a small Norman ring-work has ruined the small hall and store house belonging to the chief. It may be that it is to the smaller Iron Age forts that we should look for the best evidence of Dark Age life in Wales.

OTHER AREAS

It we except the evidence for Dark Age re-occupation at Cissbury on the South Downs behind Worthing the rest of the evidence of this kind comes from the South-west. Here signs of Dark Age occupation of some kind in the form of imported Mediterranean wares have come from Cadbury Castle in South Somerset (the Camelot of legend) and also from a lesser Cadbury at Congresbury in the north of the county. The eroded coastal fort at High Peak on the Devon-Dorset boundary has also yielded some of the same material. In some cases, as presumably at Cissbury, this phase may have been very short-lived, but on the shifting frontiers of Wessex during the two centuries of westward expansion the possibilities are much greater and must be firmly borne in mind by field workers.

THE COMING OF THE NORTHMEN

In the 9th century many parts of the British Isles suffered in varying degree from raids coming initially from Norway and later from Denmark of such intensity that after the middle of the century much of the Anglo-Saxon area had been more or less brought under subjection. Various reasons have been given for the general onslaught from the North on many parts of Western Europe during the decline of the Carolingian Empire. It has been suggested that it might not have occurred had the rising kingdoms of Scandinavia remained in strong hands and the loss of central control in Denmark after the death of Horik in 854 is quoted as a particular reason for intensified raiding. A wide prospect for plunder and even settlement was certainly opened by the weakness of the successors of Charlemagne, but the attacks could only be made chiefly because of great technical advances in ship-building and seamanship in the North during the preceding century. The skilful application of sail to well-designed boats able to keep the open sea made speedy and unexpected raids by commando-like groups of sea raiders possible all round the coasts of Western Europe. There is no reason to believe that the forces engaged were very large in the 9th century, but the swift movement and determined purpose of a few raiders had a disproportionately large effect among communities ill prepared to meet this kind of threat. Plunder was the initial object and the idea of making new settle-ments came later, only taking hold in England after 850. In 865 the arrival of the so-called "Great Army" *(micel here)* under Ivar and Halfdan, the sons of Ragnar Lodbrok, was a major event. East Anglia was over-run, York fell, Northumbria became a tributary state and Mercia was brought to the verge of collapse. In 870 the raiders moved to Reading and threatened Wessex. It was now that Alfred became king in the middle of a desperate struggle. By great exertions he was able to maintain the independence of Wessex, but this was only achieved at the expense of creating two spheres of influence, Wessex and the Danelaw to the north and east of a frontier based mainly on the line of Watling Street. Alfred was able to hold his ground with some difficulty for the rest of his life and it remained for his successors to organise a successful offensive and master the intruders.

The process of settlement began earlier in the North. The creation of Norse kingdoms in Ireland and the Isle of Man was followed after 800 by the imposition of new settlers and rulers on the Orkneys and Shetlands, the coasts of Caithness and Sutherland and many of the Western Islands. A new dynasty of Orkney earls began a series of efforts to extend their rule in the north of Scotland while the Norse kings of Dublin troubled the south-west. In Southern Britain outposts were seized in Pembroke, Anglesey and the Wirral peninsula, while Cumbria received many Norse settlers.

A new phase in British history was beginning, but since it had not gone far when our period closes we have confined ourselves to showing no more than certain battle sites and other localities connected with the early phase of the struggle against the Northmen. No attempt is being made to show the extent of their settlement and the whole of the Scandinavian phase in British history is reserved for treatment on another map of this series.

NAMES AND LETTERING

The lettering used in this second edition is the same both in type and conventional meaning as that used in the first. There are two classes, upright and sloping, with the capitals proper to each. Anglo-Saxon names are shown in the upright characters, irrespective of their derivation, whether Saxon, Celtic, or unknown. Celtic names are shown in sloping characters. Names, whether Anglo-Saxon or Celtic, derived from manuscripts written after 1066, are placed within round brackets.

One, and only one, exception to this rule has been made in the case of names derived from the British Museum Harleian manuscript 3859, containing the so-called Annales Cambriae and the Historia Brittonum attributed to Nennius. This manuscript was written in the 12th century but the contents date from 954 to 955 and are certainly not later than 988 according to the best authority (Egerton Phillimore in *Y Cymmrodorion*, 1892, XI., 139). The place names from this manuscript have not been placed within brackets. Though written down late the forms are early, and in this case a literal observance of the rule would be pedantic.

Certain conventions have been adopted to distinguish other forms used. Whenever available Latin forms have been added in upright characters within square brackets. This procedure is justified by the fact that Latin names constantly occur in the documents of the period. Moreover they reflect the last departing rays of the setting sun of Rome — or at any rate they are an ecclesiastical reflection of that light, dim and faint perhaps, but authentic — the light of human progress.

Where it has been necessary to restore the original form, that form is preceded by an asterisk. Such restorations are occasionally justified when the correct form, or the nominative case, is not in doubt. Sometimes, however, when the manuscript is good, the form there used has been adopted in preference to a restoration, even when such restoration might have been regarded as legitimate. It is often very difficult to be sure of the nominative case of names which occur only in an oblique case. There is the further difficulty that some place names were regularly used in conjunction with pre-positions (e.g. *monasterium quod dicitur in Berecingum; provincia quae vocatur in Undalum;* all of these from Bede). Here the somewhat awkward form has necessarily been used because it was the one current at the time.

In Scotland the names are practically all Celtic or pre-Celtic, but the few names in upright characters, mostly from Bede, serve to indicate the extent of his knowledge and also, to some extent, the degree of penetration of Anglian culture.

No attempt has been made to standardise spellings during the period covered, nor indeed was there any standardisation until a much later date. To make any such attempt would therefore be historically unsound. The letters "u" and "w" were interchangeable in Anglo-Saxon so that such names as Huicca wudu and Hwicce are both permissible. So also with the division, or absence thereof, between words which was quite arbitrary; such names as Colenga Burna and Winterburna are both equally common.

Certain Continental forms such as Waldheim and Nhutscelle have been used because the manuscripts in which they occur, though written abroad, are the earliest in which the names occur and were actually written well within our period.

Some of the variant forms (such as Cyil and Cuil) may seem unnecessary and even pedantic. It has been considered desirable to indicate them, however, since they show that the region in which they occur was within the orbit of Anglo-Saxon knowledge, or at any rate of Bede's personal knowledge, and he was a representative of his time.

The names of the Saxon estates in Cornwall (Polltun, etc.) represent definite Teutonic influence and are therefore a fragment of history.

RIVER NAMES

The treatment of river names on the first edition of this map was based on Professor Eilert Ekwall's book *English River Names* (Oxford, 1927) and on his personal assistance in the work of classification.

A considerable number of Celtic forms of river names which appeared on the first edition have been dropped on the advice of Professor Kenneth Jackson because they were forms from Classical sources, they represent the British language of the Roman period and they are out of place on a map of Britain in the Dark Ages. Subject to this important change the practice on both editions is the same. In the case of river names the lettering used has been determined not (as in the case of other names) by the form, but by the origin. River names of Anglo-Saxon *origin* are shown in upright characters; those of non-Saxon (usually Celtic, but sometimes unknown) *origin* in sloping characters.

A large number of river names derived from manuscripts written after 1066 appear on the map. It is possible that some of these names were not given until after the end of our period. On the other hand it is certain that the majority of them go back to it, and it is probable that they were given to the rivers by the earliest settlers. It is not thought that the historical character of the map is seriously affected by the possible inclusion of a few river names which may have originated after 871.

In Scotland river names are very few. There is no collection of early forms like that of Ekwall for England and little material exists on which a study could be based.

THE CANONS OF EVIDENCE

The chief sources for the names on the map are Bede, the Anglo-Saxon (or Old English) Chronicle, contemporary charters and the Lives of the Saints including those of Germanus, Patrick, Columba, Samson, Kentigern, Cadoc, Paternus and Cuthbert. Some of the names have been taken from Asser's Life of Alfred when the sites in question are also mentioned in earlier sources. Use has also been made of the Book of Llandaff whose manuscript was written in the middle of the 12th century. Sources dating from after 871 have only been used in so far as they appear to be based upon earlier texts or to represent a genuine tradition. Thus the *Historia Regum* of Symeon of Durham has been used because it incorporates a set of 8th century Northumbrian Annals, but the names have been placed in round brackets. On the other hand the *Liber Eliensis* has not been used because the work as a whole has never been critically edited and the degree of confidence to be given to several documents and traditions which it contains has therefore never been determined. Some other sources have been passed over for the same reason.

It has been impossible to find room on the map for all the places mentioned in non-literary sources relating to this period. Many of them were only small estates which had no particular significance in the life of the time. The names of large regions and provinces have been written across the areas covered, but the precise boundaries have not been shown because they are rarely if ever known, and because they were constantly changing through the period.

The extensive study of place names which has gone on in England enables the question of early forms valid within the period of this map to be settled with some confidence, but it is otherwise in Scotland. The materials still do not exist for mapping the distribution of different types of names. For the Anglian element, which has been comparatively neglected, hardly any material has been collected. A glance at the modern map is sufficient to show that certain early types of Anglian place names occur with considerable frequency in the Lothian district where Anglian culture was strongest. But for mapping such a distribution not only would the early forms be required, but also an investigation of adjacent regions where they may occur, such as Fife, Angus and south-west Dumfriesshire.

BIBLIOGRAPHY

Adamnan ... ... *Life of St. Columba*, edited and translated by A.O. and M.O. Anderson, Edinburgh, 1961.

Allen, J. Romilly and
Joseph Anderson ... ... *The Early Christian Monuments of Scotland*, Edinburgh, 1903.

Anglo-Saxon Chronicle, The ... edited by D. Whitelock, D.C. Douglas and S.I. Tucker, London, 1961.

Baldwin Brown, G. ... ... *The Arts in Early England*, 5 vols., London, 1921-26.

Bede ... ... *A History of the English Church and People*, translated by Leo Sherley-Price, Penguin Classics, 1957.

Blair, P.H. ... ... *An Introduction to Anglo-Saxon England*, Cambridge, 1962.

Chadwick, H.M. ... ... *The Origin of the English Nation*, Cambridge, 1924.

Chadwick, H.M. ... ... *Early Scotland*, Cambridge, 1949.

Chadwick, Nora K. ... ... *Celtic Britain*, London, 1964.

Chadwick, Nora K. *(editor)* ... *Studies in Early British History*, Cambridge, 1959.

Chadwick, Nora K. *(editor)* ... *Celt and Saxon: Studies in the Early British Border*, Cambridge, 1963.

Collingwood, W.G. ... ... *Northumbrian Crosses of the pre-Norman Age*, London, 1927.
Collingwood, R.G. and
Myres, J.N.L. ... ... *Roman Britain and the English Settlements*, 2nd edition, Oxford, 1937.

Copley, Gordon ... ... *The Conquest of Wessex in the 6th Century*, London, 1954.

Fox, C. ... ... *Offa's Dyke*, The British Academy, London, 1955.

Gildas ... ... *De Excidio Britanniae:* edited and translated by H. Williams, London, 1899.

Hamilton, J.R.C. ... ... *Jarlshof*, H.M.S.O., Edinburgh, 1953.

Harden, D.B. *(editor)* ... ... *Dark-Age Britain*, studies presented to E.T. Leeds, London, 1956.

Hencken, H.O'N. ... ... *The Archaeology of Cornwall and Scilly*, London, 1932.

Jackson, K. ... ... *Language and History in Early Britain*, Edinburgh, 1953.

Kendrick, T.D. ... ... *Anglo-Saxon Art*, London, 1938.

Lloyd, J.E. ... ... *The History of Wales*, 2 vols., 3rd edition, London, 1939.

Macalister, R.A.S. ... ... *Corpus Inscriptionum Insularum Celticarum*, vol. I, Dublin, 1945; vol. II, Dublin, 1949.

Meaney, Audrey S. ... ... *Gazetteer of Early Anglo-Saxon Burial Sites*, London, 1963.

Nash Williams, V.E. ... ... *The Early Christian Monuments of Wales*, Cardiff, 1950.

Nennius ... ... *Historia Britonum, Monumenta Historica Britannica*, edited T.D. Hardy, London, 1848; also edited by T. Mommsen in *Monumenta Germaniae Historica*, Berlin, 1894 and by F. Lot, Paris, 1934.

Phillips, C.W. ... ... *The Excavation of the Sutton Hoo Ship-burial*, Antiquaries' Journal, vol. XX, 1940 p.p. 147 - 202.

Stenton, F.M. ... ... *Anglo-Saxon England*, Oxford, 2nd edition, 1947.

Taylor, H.M. and Joan ... *Anglo-Saxon Architecture*, Cambridge, 1965.

Wade-Evans, A.W. ... ... *Nennius's History of the Britons*, London, 1938.

Wainwright, F.T. *(editor)* ... *The Problem of the Picts*, Edinburgh, 1955.

Whitelock, Dorothy ... ... *The Beginnings of English Society*, Pelican Books, 1952.

Wilson, D.M. ... ... *The Anglo-Saxons*, London, 1960.

PRELIMINARY NOTE TO INDEX

The different types of feature shown on the map are listed separately in this index.

In some cases, and in particular with the various types of Anglo-Saxon burial, it is only possible to assign a given example to a list on the basis of the information possessed. This may be defective owing to inaccurate reporting or to the probability that the cemetery in question was, for one reason or another, incompletely explored. Thus the true balance of the types of burial represented may not be known. Users may have formed their own opinion in any given case. If, therefore, a cemetery is expected in the "Predominantly inhumation" class and it is not there a search should be made in the "Mixed inhumation-cremation" list, and so on. It is hoped that in one way and another practically all known burials have been drawn in, but classification according to the user's expectation cannot be guaranteed.

The first entry in connection with any feature is the name of the parish in which it occurs. It is unfortunate that sometimes wrong attributions of parish have been given to finds in the literature and these have become firmly associated with them. We have attempted a strict adherence to the truth and it may therefore be that users looking for a familiar parish name may not find it, though the second column, giving the distinctive name of the feature where it has one, will often set them on the right path.

The question whether many seventh century Anglo-Saxon burials are pagan or Christian is sometimes an open one. An attempt has been made to indicate these cases by prefixing an asterisk (*) to these entries in the lists.

Each list contains five columns:—

Column 1 gives the name of the parish in which the feature occurs. It is in full alphabetical order.

Column 2 gives the distinctive name, if any, by which it is known, or any other succinct information which may lead to its easier identification. Many features have never been known by their parish name and in these cases a cross-reference is provided.

Column 3 gives the National Grid references of each feature to six figures. In a limited number of cases only four figures are supplied where the precise position is in doubt.

Column 4 contains an abbreviated form of the name of the county in which the item occurs. Now that the National Grid series of the Six-inch maps is well on its way to completion there is no longer any point in quoting the old County Series sheet number.

Column 5 gives the relevant One-inch sheet number.

CONTENTS OF INDEX

INDEX

PREDOMINANTLY INHUMATION CEMETERIES (*Possibly Christian)

PREDOMINANTLY INHUMATION CEMETERIES—(Continued)

Parish	Distinctive Name	Grid Reference	County	One-inch Sheet No.
Exning	Windmill Hill	TL625658	Suffolk	135
Eynsham	Housing estate	SP433099	Oxon	158
Fairford	Waterslade	SP145015	Glos	157
Fancott	Brickworks	TL018279	Beds	147
Fareham	Clapper Hill, Wallington	SU590075	Hants	180
Farningham	Charton Manor	TQ555665	Kent	171
Farthing Down, *see* Coulsdon				
Faversham	King's Field	TR013609	Kent	172
Feering	near Kelvedon Station	TL868192	Essex	149
Fen Ditton	Fleam Dyke	TL507594	Cambs	135
Ferring	Highdown Hill	TQ092043	Sussex	182
Fetcham	Hawk's Hill	TQ155554	Surrey	170
Fetcham	Watersmeet	TQ160567	Surrey	170
Filkins	Purbrick's Close	SP237043	Oxon	157
Finglesham, *see* Northbourne				
Folkestone	Dover Hill	TR238376	Kent	173
Fonaby, *see* Caistor on the Wolds				
Fornham St. Genevieve		TL834690	Suffolk	136
Foulden		TL781994	Norfolk	136
*Garton on the Wolds	Green Lane crossing	SE988577	Yorks	98
Garton on the Wolds	Sykes Memorial	SE936617	Yorks	98
Gerpins, *see* Rainham				
Gilton, *see* Ash				
Glaston	Sand pit	SK894005	Rutland	122
Glynde	Balcombe Pit	TQ460084	Sussex	183
Goodmanham		SE889431	Yorks	98
Great Addington	Shooter's Hill	SP957744	Northants	134
Great Bedwyn	Crofton pumping station	SU261623	Wilts	167
Greenwich	Old Tilt Yard	TQ387778	Kent	161
Grendon		SP879604	Northants	133
Grimstone End, *see* Pakenham				
Guildford	Mareschal Road	SU992492	Surrey	170
Guildford	Guildown	SU988488	Surrey	170
Halford	Halford Bridge	SP259453	Warw	144
Hanwell	County Schools	TQ159798	Midd	170
Harrold		SP954572	Beds	133
Hartwell		SP791125	Bucks	146
Harwell		SU489882	Berks	158
Hathern, *see* Sutton Bonington				
Hauxton		TL432528	Cambs	148
Hawk's Hill, *see* Fetcham				
Higham	Hoo Junction	TQ703736	Kent	172
Highdown Hill, *see* Ferring				
Holborough Hill, *see* Snodland				
Holkham	Howe Hill	TF877450	Norfolk	125
Holme Pierrepont		SK625391	Notts	112
*Holywell Row	Snell's Corner	TL714765	Suffolk	135
*Horndean		SU707153	Hants	181
Hornsea		TA207484	Yorks	99
Horton Kirby		TQ564694	Kent	171
Houghton Regis	Puddlehill	TL003237	Beds	147
Howick	Howick Heugh	NU236168	Northum	71

Parish	Distinctive Name	Grid Reference	County	One-inch Sheet No.
Howletts, *see* Littlebourne				
Hunstanton	Hunstanton **Park**	TF695411	Norfolk	124
Icklingham	Mitchell's Hill	TL778723	Suffolk	136
Idbury	Idbury Camp	SP226195	Oxon	144
Irby on Humber	Welbeck Hill	TA219041	Linc	105
Islip	Islip Ironworks	SP986790	Northants	134
Ixworth	Cross House	TL935701	Suffolk	136
Kemble	Clayfurlong Farm	ST989978	Glos	157
Kemble		ST971966	Glos	157
Kenninghall		TM034861	Norfolk	136
Kilham	Tuft Hill	TA079519	Yorks	93
Kineton	Pittern Hill	SP326516	Warw	144
King's Field, *see* Faversham				
King's Sutton	Burton Farm	SP515370	Northants	145
Kingston by Lewes	"Saxonbury"	TQ407095	Sussex	183
Kirkburn	Driffield Aerodrome	TA000560	Yorks	98, 99
Laceby		TA203066	Linc	105
Lakenheath	Aerodrome Hospital	TL731803	Suffolk	135
Lancing	How Court	TQ190060	Sussex	182
Leamington	Emscote	SP306652	Warw	132
Leighton Buzzard	Chamberlain's Barn	SP927263	Beds	146
Letchworth	Blackhorse Road	TL233336	Herts	147
Lighthorne		SP335562	Warw	132
Linton		TL583468	Cambs	148
Littlebourne	Howletts	TR200568	Kent	173
Little Shelford		TL459509	Cambs	148
Londesbrough		SE871462	Yorks	98
Long Compton	Little Rollright	SP296310	Warw	145
Lower Heyford	Grass Seeds Field	SP488245	Oxon	145
Luton	Argyll Avenue	TL081229	Beds	147
Lydiard Tregoze	Bassett Down House	SU115799	Wilts	157
Lyminge		TR163416	Kent	173
Lyminge	Railway site	TR167407	Kent	173
Lyneham	Lyneham Camp	SP297210	Oxon	145
Maidstone	Wheeler Street	TQ763561	Kent	172
Margate	St. John's Cemetery	TR349691	Kent	173
Margate	Gas Alley	TR357708	Kent	173
*Melbourn	Street Way	TL382438	Cambs	147
Melton Mowbray		SK756194	Leic	122
Mentmore		SP906196	Bucks	146
Micheldever	Weston	SU505396	Hants	168
Milton next	North Field	SU487925	Berks	158
Milton next Sittingbourne	Fair Meadows	TQ905640	Kent	172
Minster Lovell		SP317110	Oxon	145
Minster in Thanet		TR317634	Kent	173
Mitcham	Dead Man's Close	TQ270681	Surrey	170
Mundford		TL799934	Norfolk	136
Nettleton		TA111007	Linc	104
Newnham		SP595596	Northants	132
Newport Pagnell		SP887453	Bucks	146
Newport Pagnell	Tickfordfield Farm	SP887442	Bucks	146
*Newton and Biggin	Newton Lodge	SP530780	Warw	132
Noah's Ark, *see* Cookham				

PREDOMINANTLY INHUMATION CEMETERIES—(Continued)

Parish	Distinctive Name	Grid Reference	County	One-inch Sheet No.
Northbourne	Finglesham	TR325534	Kent	173
*North Leigh	...	SP387143	Oxon	145
North Newbald	Sand pit	SE909368	Yorks	98
North Runcton	Churchyard	TF646159	Norfolk	124
Northwold	Watermill	TL770961	Norfolk	136
Norton	Watling Street	SP619658	Northants	133
Oakington	...	TL415645	Cambs	135
Oddington	Rectory	SP553152	Oxon	146
Ogbourne St. Andrew	Barbury Castle	SU150763	Wilts	157
Ozengell, *see* Ramsgate				
Pakenham	Grimstone End	TL936693	Suffolk	136
Partney	...	TR410684	Linc	114
Patrixbourne	above Patrixbourne Church	TR199548	Kent	173
Patrixbourne	Bifrons	TR199545	Kent	173
Peterborough	...	TL185975	Northants	134
Peter's Finger, *see* Salisbury				
Portslade	Church Road	TQ259052	Sussex	182
Prittlewell	...	TQ878873	Essex	162
Puddlehill, *see* Houghton Regis				
Purton	Fox Inn	SU108874	Wilts	157
Purwell Farm, *see* Cassington				
Pyecombe	Wolstonbury Hill	TQ284138	Sussex	182
Rainham	Gerpins	TQ553836	Essex	161
Ramsgate	St. Augustine's College	TR361645	Kent	173
Remenham	Aston	SU783842	Berks	159
Rochester	Gordon Terrace	TQ746680	Kent	172
Rochester	Star Hill	TQ747680	Kent	172
Rothley Temple	...	SK568122	Leic	121
Ruskington	...	TF076513	Linc	113
Saffron Walden	Paille Ditches	TL533382	Essex	148
Salisbury, Clarendon Park	Peter's Finger	SU163290	Wilts	167
Salisbury	St. Edmund's Church	SU147304	Wilts	167
Saltford	Avon Farm	ST686686	Somerset	156
Sancton	...	SE903402	Yorks	98
Sanderstead	...	TQ331624	Surrey	170
*Sarre	...	TR261650	Kent	173
Sawston	Huckeridge Hill	TL480504	Cambs	148
Scotter	School site	SE886005	Linc	104
Seamer	Seamer Moor	TA028841	Yorks	93
Searby	...	TA073060	Linc	104
Selmeston	near Church Farm	TQ510070	Sussex	183
Sewerby cum Marton	...	TA205691	Yorks	93
Shepperton	Warre Close	TQ080667	Midd	170
Sherrington	Long barrow	ST968391	Wilts	167
Shoreham on Sea	Mill Hill	TQ214065	Sussex	182
*Shudy Camps	...	TL605444	Cambs	148
Smith's Pit II, *see* Cassington				
Snell's Corner, *see* Horndean				
Snodland	Holborough Hill	TQ698626	Kent	171
Snodland	Parrington's Lane	TQ701627	Kent	171
Soham	New cemetery site	TL599723	Cambs	135
Soham	Parish church site	TL593731	Cambs	135
Soham	Waterworks site	TL614716	Cambs	135
Southampton	St. Mary's Chapel	SU428117	Hants	180
South Malling	Malling Hill	TQ421112	Sussex	183
South Witham	Witham Common	SK937200	Linc	122
Sporle	Petygards Farm	TF885075	Norfolk	125
*Standlake	Standlake Down	SP386046	Oxon	158
Stanton Harcourt	Barrow Field	SP411051	Oxon	158
Stapenhill	...	SK257212	Staf	120
Stone	...	SP779122	Bucks	146
*Stowting	...	TR123423	Kent	173
Strood	Temple Farm	TQ732687	Kent	172
Sutton Bonington	Hathern Station	SK515241	Notts	121
Sutton Courtenay	Amey's gravel pit	SU510945	Berks	158
Sysonby	...	SK738189	Leic	122
Tetford	Tetford Hill	TF334760	Linc	105
Teynham	...	TQ956637	Kent	172
Thenford	...	SP527435	Northants	145
Thetford	...	TL864825	Norfolk	136
Thorndon	White House Farm	TM136701	Norfolk	136
Thurnham	Thurnham Friars	TF723425	Kent	172
Thurnham	Sheepwalk Hill	TQ806578	Kent	172
Toddington	...	TL013292	Beds	147
Tremenworth Down, *see* Crundale				
Trumpington	Dam Hill	TL450550	Cambs	148
Twywell, *see* Cranston				
Uffington	White Horse Hill	SU300865	Berks	158
*Uncleby	...	SE821594	Yorks	98
Upchurch	Otterham Creek	TQ828671	Kent	172
Upper Wichendon	Eythrope	SP771141	Bucks	146
Upton Snodsbury	...	SO944544	Worc	144
Valetta House, *see* Broadstairs				
Waddington	...	SK976640	Linc	113
Wanborough	Fox Hill	SU224820	Wilts	157
Warminster	Battlesbury Camp	ST898456	Wilts	166
Warwick	Longbridge Park	SP275632	Warw	131
Watton	...	TL919007	Norfolk	136
Welton	...	SP570664	Northants	133
Wickhambreux	Supperton	TR227604	Kent	173
Wigston Magna	...	SP608978	Leic	133
Willoughby on the Wolds	Foss crossroads	SK650252	Leic	122
Winceby	Roundhills	TF311695	Linc	114
*Winchester	Winnall Estate	SU494302	Hants	168
Winchester	St. Giles' Hill	SU489292	Hants	168
Winchester	West Hill	SU472295	Hants	168
Wingham	Witherden Farm	TR249569	Kent	173
Winnall, *see* Winchester				
Winterbourne Gunner	Thorny Down Road	SU182352	Wilts	167
Winterslow	Roche Court Down	SU251357	Wilts	167
Winterslow	...	SU250350	Wilts	167
Woodingdean, *see* Brighton				
Woodnesborough	...	TR308568	Kent	173

PREDOMINANTLY INHUMATION CEMETERIES—(Continued)

Parish	Distinctive Name	Grid Reference	County	One-inch Sheet No.
Woodston		TL177975	Hunts	134
Woolsthorpe by Belvoir	Sewestern Lane	SK847333	Linc	122
Wrotham	Pumping station site	TQ620590	Kent	171
Wychnor		SK194159	Staf	120
Wytham		SP468098	Berks	145
Yarnton		SP476114	Oxon	145
Yeavering		NY925305	Northum	64
Yelford	Westfield Farm	SP369049	Oxon	158

PREDOMINANTLY CREMATION CEMETERIES

Parish	Distinctive Name	Grid Reference	County	One-inch Sheet No.
Ancaster		SK983423	Linc	113
Baston	Tinker's Hurn	TF110137	Linc	123
Brettenham	Shadwell	TL935834	Norfolk	136
Brooke		TM294995	Norfolk	137
Broughton		SE771728	Yorks	92
Brundall	Brundall Gardens	TG317085	Norfolk	126
Bungay	Stow Park	TM327879	Suffolk	137
Burgh Castle		TG476045	Suffolk	126
Burton Stather	Bagmoor	SE904171	Linc	104
Caistor St. Edmunds		TG235032	Norfolk	126
Cambridge St. Giles				
Castle Acre	Priory Field	TF797156	Norfolk	125
Drayton	Drayton Lodge	TG188131	Norfolk	126
Dunsley, see Newholm cum Dunsley				
Earsham		TM326888	Norfolk	137
Eye		TM156748	Suffolk	136
Fareham	North Turnpike	SU576065	Hants	180
Finningham	Railway site	TM066684	Suffolk	136
Grantham		SK920349	Linc	113
Great Walsingham	Spittlegate	TF938575	Norfolk	125
Heworth		SE610529	Yorks	97
Hibaldstow		SE960030	Linc	104
Hough on the Hill	Loveden Hill	SK907458	Linc	113
Illington, see Wretham				
Kettering	Stamford Road	SP876792	Northants	133
King's Newton, see Melbourne				
Kingston on Soar		SK502277	Notts	121
Kirton in Lindsey		SK938007	Linc	104
Lackford	Mill Heath	TL776713	Suffolk	136
Little Paxton		TL193628	Hunts	134
Loveden Hill, see Hough on the Hill				
Mannington, see Wolterton				
Markshall		TG229939	Norfolk	126
Melbourne	King's Newton	SK390260	Derby	120
Narford	Bradmoor	TF773145	Norfolk	125
Newark on Trent	Millgate	SK793336	Notts	112-3
Newholm cum Dunsley	Dunsley	NZ858111	Yorks	86
North Elmham	Spong Hill	TF983195	Norfolk	125
Norwich	Eade Road	TG227099	Norfolk	126
Pitsford		SP747684	Northants	133
Redgrave	Moneypot Hill	TM046787	Suffolk	136
Rendlesham	Hoo Hill	TM331535	Suffolk	150
Rockland All Saints	Mount Pleasant	TL994948	Norfolk	136
St. Giles, Cambridge	Strange's Boathouse	TL448192	Cambs	135
St. Neots	Avenue Road, East Street	TL187605	Hunts	134
Sancton		SE903402	Yorks	98
Sandy	Railway Bridge site	TL177488	Beds	147
Sedgeford	Sedgeford Hall	TF717357	Norfolk	124
Shefford		TL135387	Beds	147
Shropham		TL992910	Norfolk	136
Snape		TM402597	Suffolk	137
South Elkington	Cow Pasture Farm	TF312883	Linc	105
South Willingham		TF200830	Linc	105
Spong Hill, see North Elmham				

MIXED INHUMATION-CREMATION CEMETERIES (*Possibly Christian)

Parish	Distinctive Name	Grid Reference	County	One-inch Sheet No.
Abingdon	Caldecott	SU490963	Berks	158
Alveston		SP210547	Warw	144
Badwell Ash		TM002693	Suffolk	136
Baginton		SP348748	Warw	132
Barkby	Barkby Field	SK636098	Leic	121
Barrington	Hooper's Field	TL387497	Cambs	148
Barton under Needwood		SK205182	Staf	120
Barton Seagrave	Barton and Walton Station	SP887773	Northants	133
Beddington		TQ300654	Surrey	170
Bidford on Avon		SP099918	Warw	144
Bledlow	The Cop	SP774010	Bucks	159
Brighthampton	Malthouse Farm	SP383033	Oxon	158
Brixworth (2)		SP747720	Northants	133
Brundall	St. Clement site	TG330079	Norfolk	126
Cambridge	St. John's Cricket Ground	TL441188	Cambs	135
Caythorpe	Rose Crescent	SK940470	Linc	113
Chessell Down, see Shalfleet				
*Desborough (2)		SP800840 / SP805830	Northants	133
Driffield	Railway siding	TA029574	Yorks	99
Duston	Noah's Ark	SP726602	Northants	133
Frilford		SU437964	Berks	158
Girton	Girton College	TL423609	Cambs	135
Glen Parva	Blaby Railway Station	SP569987	Leic	132
Glynde	Ringmer Road	TQ449111	Sussex	183

MIXED INHUMATION-CREMATION CEMETERIES—(Continued)

Parish	Distinctive Name	Grid Reference	County	One-inch Sheet No.
Great Chesterford	...	TL501435	Essex	148
Hampnett	...	SP105151	Glos	144
Hargham	...	TM019913	Norfolk	136
Hartford	Cantelupe Farm...	TL254727	Hunts	134
Haslingfield	...	TL413530	Cambs	148
Hassocks	...	TQ296155	Sussex	182
Heckington	Butts Hill	TF141437	Linc	113
Hildersham	Furrey Hills	TL552487	Cambs	148
Holdenby	Coneybury Hill	SP695671	Northants	133
Horton Kirby...	Riseley	TQ563676	Kent	171
*Ipswich	Hadleigh Road	TM146445	Suffolk	150
*Kempston	Long Lane	TL031474	Beds	147
Kettlestone	...	TF950295	Norfolk	125
Kingsey	Tythrop Park	SP741072	Oxon	159
King's Worthy	Worthy Park	SU500328	Hants	168
Knipton	...	SK823311	Leic	122
Lakenheath	...	TL729830	Suffolk	135
Leicester	Rowley Fields	SK571019	Leic	121
*Leighton Buzzard	Deadman's Slade	SP921265	Beds	146
Linton...	...	TL564468	Cambs	135
Little Wilbraham	Streetway Hill	SU560577	Cambs	135
*Long Wittenham	...	SU545937	Berks	158
Market Overton	Land Close Field	SK900170	Rutland	122
Marston St. Lawrence	Marston Hill Farm	SP542439	Northants	145
*Mildenhall	Warren Hill	TL745741	Suffolk	135
Nafferton	Nafferton Brickyard	TA060587	Yorks	99
Nassington	St. Andrew's Hospital	TL071916	Northants	134
Northampton	...	SP770605	Northants	133
Northfleet	...	TQ622738	Kent	171
North Luffenham	...	SK932045	Rutland	122
Pensthorpe, see Kettlestone, Long Lane				
Reading	"Dreadnought" site	SU741739	Berks	159
Ringmer	...	TQ449111	Sussex	183
Robin Hood's Bay	...	NZ948052	Yorks	93
Rothwell	...	SP815810	Northants	133
St. John's Cricket Ground, see Cambridge				
Saltburn on Sea	...	NZ651205	Yorks	86
*Saxby	Stapleford Park...	SK814193	Leic	122
Shalfleet	Chessell Down...	SZ399813	Hants	180
Shepperton	Upper West Field	TQ067673	Midd	170
Shepperton	Walton Bridge Green	TQ092665	Midd	170
Sleaford	Sleaford Station...	TF066454	Linc	113
Souldern	...	SP519314	Oxon	145
Stamford	...	TF041076	Linc	123
Stapleford Park, see Saxby				
Sudborough	...	SP967821	Northants	134
Thealby	...	SE904172	Linc	104
Toddington	Bagmoor Mine...	TL002283	Beds	147
Tottenhill	Warmark	TF635108	Norfolk	124
Tuddenham	...	TL741704	Suffolk	135
Ufford	...	TM294520	Suffolk	150
Upper Dunsforth	Devil Cross	SE426633	Yorks	91

Parish	Distinctive Name	Grid Reference	County	One-inch Sheet No.
Wallingford	St. John's Road	SU604890	Berks	158
Warmark, see Toddington				
*Westbere	...	TR199615	Kent	173
West Stow	West Stow Heath	TL795714	Suffolk	136
Wheatley	...	SP602046	Oxon	158
Wigston Magna	Kirkdale Close	SP380981	Leic	132

PRIMARY BARROW BURIALS BY INHUMATION (*Possibly Christian)

Parish	Distinctive Name	Grid Reference	County	One-inch Sheet No.
Alciston	Alciston Front Hill	TQ490056	Sussex	183
Alstonefield	Stand Low	SK138536	Staf	111
Alvediston	Middle Down	ST967252	Wilts	167
Aston Upthorpe	Lowbury...	SU541823	Berks	158
*Barfriston	Sibertswold	TR266488	Kent	173
*Barham	Breach Downs	TR205485	Kent	173
Bekesbourne	Cowslip Wood	TR207548	Kent	173
Benty Grange, see Hartington Middle Quarter				
Bishopsbourne	Bourne Park	TR191530	Kent	173
Bottisham	Allington Hill	TL576590	Cambs	135
Bower Chalke...	...	SU0220	Wilts	161
Breach Downs, see Barham				
Brushfield	Lapwing Hill	SK166717	Derby	111
Brushfield	Cock Hill	SK168723	Derby	111
Burgh le Marsh	Friday's Church	TF499650	Linc	114
Burpham	Perry Hill	TQ065098	Sussex	182
Burpham	...	TQ055094	Sussex	182
Caenby	...	SK970889	Linc	104
Carisbrooke	Bowcombe Down	SZ461874	Hants	180
*Chartham	Swadling Down...	TR108542	Kent	173
Chatham	Chatham Lines	TQ764681	Kent	172
*Chelmorton	Chelmorton Thorn	SK118694	Derby	111
Clapham	Newbarn Down...	TQ084091	Sussex	182
Compton Verney	...	SP310528	Warw	145
Cookham	...	SU890870	Berks	159
Coombe Bissett	Salisbury Racecourse	SU103281	Wilts	167
Coulsdon	Farthing Down	TQ299983	Surrey	170
*Edlaston and Wyaston	Wyaston	SK191424	Derby	120
*Elton	White Low	SK225598	Derby	111
Farthing Down, see Coulsdon				
Glynde	Saxon Down	TQ444103	Sussex	183
Golgotha, see Barfriston, Sibertswold				
Greenwich	Greenwich Park...	TQ387773	Kent	171
Harnsey	...	TQ392119	Sussex	183
*Hartington	Hurdlow...	SK117666	Derby	111
Hartington Middle Quarter	Benty Grange	SK146642	Derby	111
*Hartington Upper Quarter	Great Low	SK105682	Derby	111
Hawnby	Sunny Bank	SE527892	Yorks	92
Heddington	King's Play Down	SU000659	Wilts	157
Hough on the Hill	Loveden Hill	SK907458	Linc	113
Hurdlow, see Hartington Middle Quarter				

PRIMARY BARROW BURIALS BY INHUMATION—(Continued)

Parish	Distinctive Name	Grid Reference	County	One-inch Sheet No.
*Kingston	Kingston Down...	TR202319	Kent	173
Loveden Hill, *see* Hough on the Hill				
Maiden Bradley	Rodmead Down	ST819360	Wilts	166
Martlesham		TM245461	Suffolk	150
Middleton and Smerrill	Cross Flatts	SK192637	Derby	111
Middleton and Smerrill	Long Gallery Plantation	SK185615	Derby	111
Middleton by Wirksworth		SK268556	Derby	111
*Newton Grange	Stand Low	SK160930	Derby	111
Northampton	Cow Meadow	SP758600	Northants	133
Partney		TF422681	Linc	114
Ramshorn	Wredon Hill	SK085467	Staf	111
Rodmell	Mill Hill	TQ413053	Sussex	183
*Roundway	Roundway Down	SU000650	Wilts	167
Sibertswold, *see* Barfriston				
Stenigot		TF253822	Linc	105
Stodmarsh		TR215603	Kent	173
Stoke Golding		SP396970	Leic	132
Sullington	Sullington Hill	TQ094120	Sussex	182
Swadling Down, *see* Chartham				
Taplow		SU906821	Bucks	159
Temple Ewell		TR291443	Kent	173
West Firle	Firle Beacon	TQ488017	Sussex	183
West Knoyle		ST863337	Wilts	166
Winterslow	Roche Court Down	SU251357	Wilts	167
Wirksworth	Middleton Moor	SK268556	Derby	111
Woodnesborough		TR297575	Kent	173
Wye		TR069470	Kent	173

PRIMARY BARROW BURIALS BY CREMATION

Parish	Distinctive Name	Grid Reference	County	One-inch Sheet No.
Asthall	Asthall Barrow	SP289101	Oxon	145
Brightwell	Brightwell Heath	TM241444	Suffolk	150
Eaton and Alsop	near Net Low	SK148567	Derby	111
Hartington Middle Quarter	near Newhaven House	SK161602	Derby	111
Sutton	Sutton Hoo	TM287487	Suffolk	150
West Stoke	Bow Hill...	SU819098	Sussex	181
Woodnesborough	Coombe	TR298176	Kent	173
Worplesdon	Whitmoor Common	SU091537	Surrey	170

SECONDARY BARROW BURIALS BY INHUMATION (*Possibly Christian)

Parish	Distinctive Name	Grid Reference	County	One-inch Sheet No.
Alsop, *see* Eaton and Alsop, Cross Low				
Alstonefield	Stanshope	SK127542	Staf	111
Alstonefield	Steep Lowe	SK123561	Staf	111
Amesbury	Barrow 44	SU119427	Wilts	167
Amesbury	Barrow 85	SU177400	Wilts	167
Arreton	Arreton Down	SZ535874	Hants	180
Avening	Chavenage Green	ST877960	Glos	157

Parish	Distinctive Name	Grid Reference	County	One-inch Sheet No.
Ballidon	Royston Grange	SK200567	Derby	111
Ballidon	Minninglow	SK209572	Derby	111
*Ballidon	Galley Low	SK214564	Derby	111
Barnham	Barnham Heath	TL887797	Suffolk	136
Barrasford	Railway station site	NY919736	Northum	77
Barrow	Barrow Bottom	TL773661	Suffolk	136
Beddingham	Beddingham Hill	TQ459060	Sussex	183
Bedhampton	Bevis's Grave	SU692064	Hants	181
Bishopstone	Hinton Down	SU238800	Wilts	157
Bishopstrow	King Barrow	ST897444	Wilts	166
Bishop Wilton	Wilton Beacon	SE812563	Yorks	98
Bratton	Bratton Castle long barrow	ST900516	Wilts	167
Burpham	Peppering Barrow	TQ042100	Sussex	182
Calton	...	SK108502	Staf	111
Carthorpe	Howe Hill	SE309838	Yorks	91
*Cherhill (2)	Yatesbury Field	SU070709	Wilts	157
Cherry Hinton		TL484555	Cambs	135
Chinnor		SP765002	Oxon	159
Cleethorpes	Beacon Hill	TA299080	Linc	105
Clyffe Pypard		SU095777	Wilts	157
Codford St. Peter	Aston Valley	ST980428	Wilts	167
Cookham	Cock Marsh	SU886870	Berks	159
Coombes		TQ182084	Sussex	182
Cosham	Long barrow	SU667064	Hants	181
Cowlam	Kemp Howe	SE961662	Yorks	93
Crawley		SP340120	Oxon	145
Driffield	Cheesecake Hill	TA042578	Yorks	99
Driffield	Halliman's Wath Bridge	TA017566	Yorks	99
Driffield	Cricket ground	TA019574	Yorks	99
Duggleby	Duggleby Howe	SE880668	Yorks	92
Durnford	Little Down	SU133374	Wilts	167
Durrington		SU116441	Wilts	167
East Ilsley	Cross Barrows	SU506810	Berks	158
East Knoyle	Keesley Lodge	ST866338	Wilts	166
*Eaton and Alsop	Cross Low	SK163553	Derby	111
Everleigh	Everleigh Barrows	SU184560	Wilts	167
Ferrybridge	Round Hill	SE473244	Yorks	97
Fimber	Church site	SE894606	Yorks	98
Galley Low, *see* Ballidon				
Ganton	Ganton Wold	TA003761	Yorks	93
Goathland	Lilla Howe	SE889986	Yorks	92
Grafton	Great Botley Copse	SU293600	Wilts	167
*Green Fairfield	Cow Low	SK102729	Derby	111
Grind Low, *see* Overhaddon				
Hardown Hill, *see* Whitchurch Canonicorum				
Hartington Middle Quarter	Vincent Knoll, Parsley Hay	SK137635	Derby	111
Hartington Middle Quarter	near Pilsbury	SK120639	Derby	111
Hartington Middle Quarter	Waggon Low	SK116648	Derby	111
Hartington Town Quarter	Carder Low	SK128626	Derby	111
Heytesbury	Bowl's Barrow	ST942468	Wilts	167

SECONDARY BURIALS BY INHUMATION—(Continued)

Parish	Distinctive Name	Grid Reference	County	One-inch Sheet No.
Hollingbourne	Whiteheath	TQ821547	Kent	172
Houghton le Spring	Copt Hill	NZ353492	Durham	85
Idmiston	...	SU228353	Wilts	167
Ilam	Castern	SK123526	Staf	111
Kemp Howe, *see* Cowlam				
Kingthorpe	...	SE834857	Yorks	92
*Kniveton	Wigber Low	SK204514	Derby	111
Knook	Long barrow	ST936446	Wilts	167
Langham	...	TG020411	Norfolk	125
Lilla Howe, *see* Goathland				
Little Longstone	...	SK178723	Derby	111
Long Crichel	Launceston Down	ST950100	Dorset	179
Lyneham	Long barrow	SP297210	Oxon	145
Marton	Railway site	SP404681	Warw	132
Middleton and Smerrill	Rusden Low	SK191623	Derby	111
Middleton and Smerrill	Pegge's Barrow, Garrit Piece	SK171626	Derby	111
Milston	Silk Hill	SU190470	Wilts	167
Milston	...	SU190469	Wilts	167
Minninglow, *see* Ballidon				
Oddington	Martin's Hill	SP216253	Glos	144
Ogbourne St. Andrew	Churchyard barrow	SU188723	Wilts	157
Oldbury	Hartshill	SP317944	Warw	132
*Overhaddon	Grind Low	SK202669	Derby	111
Oxton	Mortimer No. 200	SE630915	Notts	112
Painsthorpe	Bloodmore Hill	SE829585	Yorks	98
Pakefield	Blackpatch	TM519897	Suffolk	137
Patching	Woodyates	TQ094088	Sussex	182
Pentridge	Woodyates	SU053181	Dorset	179
Pentridge	...	SU039195	Dorset	179
Pickering	Long Barrow Field	SE7985	Yorks	92
Preston Candover	Greenwell No. LXXVII	SU604403	Hants	168
Rudston	...	TA107665	Yorks	93
St. Margaret at Cliffe	Tennis court site	TR370460	Kent	173
St. Margaret at Cliffe	...	TR364445	Kent	173
Shalfleet	Shalcombe Down	SZ590850	Hants	180
Shillington	Pegsdon Common	TL133310	Beds	147
Sullington	Sullington Hill	TQ094120	Sussex	182
Swarkestone	Swarkestone Lows	SK366295	Derby	121
Therfield	Therfield Heath	TL340403	Herts	147
Therfield	Long barrow	TL341401	Herts	147
Tilshead	Tilshead Lodge long barrow	SU021475	Wilts	167
Tilshead	Kill Barrow long barrow	SU000478	Wilts	167
Tissington	Cromwell's Low?	SK153326	Derby	111
Tissington	Sharp Low	SK161528	Derby	111
*Tissington	Rose Low (Buslow)	SK169325	Derby	111
Upper Swell	Pole's Wood East long barrow	SP171265	Glos	144
Upper Swell	Pole's Wood South long barrow	SP167263	Glos	144
Ventnor	...	SZ556778	Hants	180
Warminster	King Barrow, Boreham	ST897444	Wilts	166
West Overton	Overton Hill	SU119683	Wilts	157
Whitchurch	Twinley Farm	SU477518	Hants	168

SECONDARY BURIALS BY INHUMATION (continued)

Parish	Distinctive Name	Grid Reference	County	One-inch Sheet No.
Whitchurch Canonicorum	Hardown Hill	SY405944	Dorset	177
Wilsford	...	SU120400	Wilts	167
Wilsford (North)	Ell Barrow	SU073513	Wilts	167
Wilsford (South)	Long barrow	SU114410	Wilts	167
Wilsford (South)	Lake barrow group	SU120395	Wilts	167
Winterbourne Stoke	Barrow 4	SU101416	Wilts	167
Winterbourne Stoke	Goddard's barrow 61	SU076420	Wilts	167
Winterslow	Winterslow Hut	SU228348	Wilts	167
Yatesbury	Barrow Field	SU070709	Wilts	157

SECONDARY BARROW BURIALS BY CREMATION

Parish	Distinctive Name	Grid Reference	County	One-inch Sheet No.
Risby	Risby Poor Heath	TL777679	Suffolk	136

INHUMATION BURIALS, UP TO THREE IN NUMBER (*Possibly Christian)

Parish	Distinctive Name	Grid Reference	County	One-inch Sheet No.
Abingdon	...	SU501976	Berks	158
Acol	...	TR308671	Kent	173
Akenham	...	TM159496	Suffolk	149
Appleton le Moors	Hepton Hill	SE729891	Yorks	92
Appleton le Street	...	SE731714	Yorks	92
Arrow	Ragley Park	SP079557	Warw	131
Ash	Richborough	TR324603	Kent	173
Ashendon	...	SP795142	Bucks	146
Ashford	...	TR010425	Kent	172
*Ashover	Overton Hall	SK347622	Derby	111
Ashtead	...	TQ200573	Surrey	170
Ashwell	Odsey	TL298386	Herts	147
Aslockton	The Barnfield	SK741404	Notts	112
Aston Cantlow	Mill Field	SP134596	Warw	131
Aston Tirrold	...	SU560860	Berks	158
Astwick	...	TL220380	Beds	147
Avebury	...	SU100700	Wilts	157
Babraham	Worstead Street	TL500530	Cambs	148
Badley	Gate Ford	TM079561	Suffolk	149
Baggrave	...	SK698090	Leic	122
Balsham	Fleam Dyke	TL570540	Cambs	148
Banstead	...	TQ241602	Surrey	170
Banstead	...	TQ247612	Surrey	170
Bardwell	...	TL943728	Suffolk	136
Barlaston	Upper House	SJ895380	Staf	110
Barnby	Wade's Stone	NZ830130	Yorks	86
Barrow upon Soar	...	SK568163	Leic	121
Barlow	near Barlow Hills	TL587449	Cambs	148
Basingstoke	West Ham	SU624519	Hants	168
Bedford	Russell Park	TL061496	Beds	147
Beeby	...	SK664082	Leic	121
Bingham	Parson's Hill	SK707403	Notts	112
Birchington	Gallwey Avenue	TR293695	Kent	173
Birchington	St. Mildred's Avenue	TR292696	Kent	173
Birstall	...	SK590090	Leic	122

Parish	Distinctive Name	Grid Reference	County	One-inch Sheet No.
East Horsley	...	TQ090520	Surrey	170
East Lockinge	Lockinge Park	SU428871	Berks	158
Eaton Socon	...	TL172603	Beds	134
Ebbesbourne Wake	Duloe Windmill	ST993254	Wilts	167
Eggington	Barrow Hill	SP960254	Beds	147
Elloughton	Gault Hill	SE941278	Yorks	98
Eriswell	Hardpiece, Foxhole Heath	TL733778	Suffolk	135
Esher	Sandown Park	TQ139650	Surrey	170
Evesham	Fairfield Housing Estate	SP040430	Worc	144
Eye	...	TF229035	Northants	123
Eynsford	Railway cutting	TQ530662	Kent	171
Faringdon	...	SU2895	Berks	158
Farley Chamberlayne	Farley Down	SU403286	Hants	168
Farndish	...	SP920630	Beds	134
Faversham	Churchyard	TR018615	Kent	172
Felixstowe	...	TM314356	Suffolk	150
Flixborough	...	SE886139	Linc	104
Foxton	...	TL408490	Cambs	148
Freckenham	...	TL666717	Suffolk	135
Frilford	Noah's Ark	SU439962	Berks	158
Friskney	...	TF4655	Linc	114
Friston	Friston Hill	TV545990	Sussex	183
Furneux Pelham	...	TL431279	Herts	148
Galewood	...	NT911323	Northum	71
Garton	west of railway station	SE978578	Yorks	98
Gillingham	Central Hotel site	TQ790687	Kent	172
Gissing	Railway	TM151850	Norfolk	136
Grantchester	...	TL431556	Cambs	135
Grantham	Flower's Brewery	SK916354	Linc	113
Grantham	...	SK926334	Linc	113
Great Cheverell	Saltersford	ST980544	Wilts	167
Great Finborough	...	TM014579	Suffolk	136
Great Oxendon	...	SP730830	Northants	133
Great Tosson	...	NU028005	Northum	71
Guston	...	TR324448	Kent	173
Hackington	Shelford Farm	TR165602	Kent	173
Hangleton	West Hove Golf Course	TQ262073	Sussex	182
Hardingstone	Hunsbury	SP737383	Northants	133
Harrietsham	...	TQ865541	Kent	172
Harrietsham	Churchyard	TQ874530	Kent	172
Headington	Pilgrims' Way	TQ873536	Oxon	158
Helpstone	Barton	SP550079	Northants	123
Henderskelfe	Castle Howard	SE716700	Yorks	92
Hepple	...	NT985006	Northum	71
Hessle	...	TA021265	Yorks	99
Hibaldstow	Castle Hill	SE960030	Linc	104
High Wycombe	...	SU866931	Bucks	159
Hilgay	...	TL622981	Norfolk	124
Hitcham	Windmill Field	SU921811	Bucks	159
Hornton	...	SP390450	Oxon	145
Horsepath	...	SP571049	Oxon	158
Hoth	Millbank	TR204652	Kent	173
Houghton	The Elms	TL287721	Hunts	134

INHUMATION BURIALS UP TO THREE IN NUMBER—(Continued)

Parish	Distinctive Name	Grid Reference	County	One-inch Sheet No.
Bishopsbourne	Bursted Wood	TR160505	Kent	173
Black Bourton	Aker's gravel pit	SP286641	Oxon	158
Bledlow	The Warren	SP775014	Bucks	159
Boughton	...	SP753658	Northants	133
Boughton Aluph	...	TR037487	Kent	172
Boynton	...	TA125674	Yorks	93
Brabourne	Iden Corner	TR104417	Kent	173
Branston	...	SK225215	Staf	120
Bretby	Brislingcote	SK273220	Derby	120
Brettenham	...	TL939845	Norfolk	136
Brize Norton	...	SP305092	Oxon	158
Broadstairs	Lindenthorpe and Stanley Roads	TR393685	Kent	173
Broadwell	Fosse Way	SP192271	Glos	144
Broome	...	TM340930	Norfolk	137
Broomfield	Clobb's Row	TL710096	Essex	161
Broughton	Broughton Hill	SU308318	Hants	168
Broughton Giffard	...	ST878622	Wilts	166
Brown Candover	...	SU580390	Hants	168
Brundall	...	TG330079	Norfolk	126
Burford	Battle Edge	SP247120	Oxon	144
*Calver	Calver Low	SK236745	Derby	111
Cambridge	Jesus Lane	TL451588	Cambs	135
Cambridge	Various	TL450580	Cambs	135
Candlesby	Reservoir site	TF455676	Linc	114
Capheaton	...	NZ017796	Northum	78
Cassington	Lay's Garage	SP445107	Oxon	145
*Castle Bytham	...	SK990180	Linc	123
Castle Eden	...	NZ420380	Durham	85
Catterick	...	SE245971	Yorks	91
Charlton All Saints	Witherington	SU184231	Wilts	167
Chesterton	Swan's gravel pit	TL475605	Cambs	135
Chilbolton	Testcombe gravel pit	SU384390	Hants	168
Chinnor	...	SP750010	Oxon	159
Cirencester	The Barton	SP016023	Glos	157
Clayton	Clayton Windmill	TQ304133	Sussex	182
Clifton Hampden	Long Hadden and Yards	SU544960	Oxon	158
Clipston	...	SP714815	Northants	133
Clopton	Meon Hill	SP173454	Warw	144
Cokethorpe	Cokethorpe Park	SP371060	Oxon	158
Coleshill	...	SU237943	Berks	157
Compton	...	SU459279	Berks	158
Corbridge	Roman site	NY982648	Northum	77
Cottesmore	...	SK902136	Rutland	122
Darenth	Darenth and Stone Hospital	TQ536739	Kent	171
Dartford	...	TQ547759	Kent	171
Daventry	Borough Hill	SP588622	Northants	132
Denton	Roman villa site	SK851324	Linc	122
Dorchester	Minchin Recreation Ground	SU577948	Oxon	158
Dorking	...	TQ160492	Surrey	170
Duffield	Duffield Castle	SK345440	Derby	120
East Boldon	...	NZ3661	Durham	78
East Garston	...	SU335877	Berks	158

INHUMATION BURIALS UP TO THREE IN NUMBER—(Continued)

Parish	Distinctive Name	Grid Reference	County	One-inch Sheet No.
Hoxne		TM190780	Suffolk	137
Hungerton	Ingarsby	SK680050	Leic	122
Hungerton		SK687062	Leic	122
Husband's Bosworth		SP648836	Leic	132
Hythe		TR158350	Kent	173
Iffley		SP530036	Oxon	158
Ippollitts	Pound Farm	TL192274	Herts	147
Irby upon Humber	Welbeck Hill	TA219041	Linc	105
Ixworth	Ixworth Thorpe	TL925720	Suffolk	136
Kempsford		SU155974	Glos	157
Kemp Town		TQ330040	Sussex	182
Kemsing		TQ547588	Kent	171
Kidlington		SP490140	Oxon	145
King's Walden	between Breachwood Green and Darley Hall	TL140220	Herts	147
Kirby Cane	Pewter Hill	TM373933	Norfolk	137
Kirtlington		SP499203	Oxon	145
Kirton in Lindsey		SK945989	Linc	104
Leagrave	Sarum Road	TL065238	Beds	147
Leckhampton	Leckhampton Hill	SO946186	Glos	144
Leeds		TQ827538	Kent	172
Leicester	Narborough Road	SK578040	Leic	121
Leicester	East Gate of Roman town	SK580040	Leic	121
Lenham	The Square	TQ898521	Kent	172
Limbury	Leagrave Marsh	TL065238	Beds	147
Little Chart	Stambers	TQ940457	Kent	172
Little Hampton		SP026431	Worc	144
Little Snoring		TF953322	Norfolk	125
Little Walsingham	Railway	TF930364	Norfolk	125
Loddington		SP810780	Northants	133
Longcot		SU279900	Berks	157
Lower Halstow		TQ856665	Kent	172
Lowesby	Lowesby Hall	SK722075	Leic	122
Luton	Dallow Road Gas Works	TL082215	Beds	147
Lympne	Bellevue	TR109349	Kent	173
Lympne	Port Lympne	TR102350	Kent	173
Market Harborough		SP737873	Leic	133
Marlborough	Savernake Hospital	SU207686	Wilts	157
Medbourne	Medbourne Field	SP794932	Leic	133
Melton		TM285506	Suffolk	150
Melton Hill		SE975268	Yorks	98
Mersham		TR050390	Kent	172
Mickleham	Juniper Hall	TQ072527	Surrey	170
Middle Wallop		SU290378	Hants	168
Milcombe		SP393357	Oxon	145
Mildenhall	Holywell Farm	TL710740	Suffolk	135
Mildenhall		SU210690	Wilts	157
Milton Regis		TQ909644	Kent	172
Milton next Sittingbourne	Brickfields	TQ920640	Kent	172
Milton next Sittingbourne	Rondean Estate	TQ900640	Kent	172
Minster	Churchyard	TR310642	Kent	173
Monkton	Primrose Hill	TR288653	Kent	173
Murston	Mere Court	TQ924646	Kent	172
Napton	Brickworks	SP455613	Warw	132
Narford		TF770140	Norfolk	125
Netheravon	Aviation School	SU156486	Wilts	167
Nether Wallop	Bradley's Farm	SU300360	Hants	168
Newington	Milky Down	TR180370	Kent	173
Newport Pagnell	Kickle's Farm	SP863448	Bucks	146
Newtimber	Summer Down	TQ269110	Sussex	182
Northampton	Harding Street	SP750610	Northants	133
North Collingham		SK846613	Notts	113
Northdown		TR380700	Kent	173
NorthElmsall		SE477127	Yorks	103
Northolt	White Hart Farm	TQ142840	Midd	160
North Tidworth	Perham Down	SU246494	Wilts	167
Norton	Chapman's Pit	TQ972591	Kent	172
Nottingham	New Baths site	SK578402	Notts	112
Oadby		SP624994	Leic	133
Occaney		SE352621	Yorks	91
Offchurch		SP380655	Warw	132
Orcheston		SU068453	Wilts	167
Ovingdean	Elston	TQ360036	Sussex	183
Oxford	Longhill	SP512078	Oxon	158
Parham	Park Crescent	TM309605	Suffolk	137
Peatling Magna	Fryer's Close	SP590920	Leic	133
Pistone		SP947148	Bucks	159
Poringland		TG271020	Norfolk	126
Poulton	Ready Token	SP105045	Glos	157
Princethorpe		SP402707	Warw	132
Purley	Railway	SU654765	Berks	158
Queen Camel		ST594255	Somerset	166
Quinton	Meon Hill	SP175454	Warw	144
Ramsgate	Station Approach Road	TR379654	Kent	173
Ramsgate	West Cliff	TR376645	Kent	173
Ramsgate	Helvellyn Avenue	TR367611	Kent	173
Reading	Workhouse site	SU698737	Berks	159
Riby		TA186078	Linc	105
Rickinghall Inferior		TM020750	Suffolk	136
Ringwould		TR350480	Kent	173
Rochester		TQ736675	Kent	172
Rottingdean	Short Bros.' Works	TQ382029	Sussex	183
Rudstone	Thorpe Hall	TA112672	Yorks	99
Rushall	Woodbridge	SU133570	Wilts	167
Sandwich		TR330380	Kent	173
Shrewton		SU065444	Wilts	167
Shrewton	Windmill site	SU060430	Wilts	167
Sittingbourne	Chalkwell	TQ894637	Kent	172
Sleaford	Mareham Lane	TF080440	Linc	113
Sleaford	Old Place	TF075458	Linc	113
Snodland	Lad's Farm	TQ686632	Kent	171
Southchurch	Thorpe Hall brickpits	TQ923857	Essex	162
Southfleet	Joyce Hall, Betsham	TQ607715	Kent	171
South Heighton		TQ453033	Sussex	183

Parish	Distinctive Name	Grid Reference	County	One-inch Sheet No.
Wickham Market	...	TM302567	Suffolk	150
Willerby	...	TA022792	Yorks	93
Winster	...	SK242605	Derby	111
Winterborne Monkton	Maiden Castle	SY671884	Dorset	178
Winterslow	Winterslow Hut.	SU234348	Wilts	167
Wisbech	Corn Exchange	TF463096	Cambs	124
Witham	Temples Field	TL818151	Essex	162
Withington	Foxcote Manor	SP012180	Glos	144
Womersley	...	SE530190	Yorks	103
Woodbridge	Haugh Lane	TM267498	Suffolk	150
Woolstone	...	SU290875	Berks	158
Wootton	...	SP479005	Berks	158
Wretton	...	TF696007	Norfolk	135
Wrotham	Bradford Platt	TQ615598	Kent	171
Wye	Church	TR070465	Kent	172
Wyre Piddle	...	SO961472	Worc	144
York	Castle Yard	SE604514	Yorks	97

SINGLE CREMATIONS

Parish	Distinctive Name	Grid Reference	County	One-inch Sheet No.
Bournemouth	Iford Bridge	SZ138933	Hants	179
Bramford	...	TM121467	Suffolk	140
Brinklow	...	SP436797	Warw	132
Culford	Cross Hall	TL833703	Suffolk	136
Eaton Socon	...	TL173615	Beds	134
Fakenham	Fakenham Heath	TL890769	Suffolk	136
Folkestone	The Bayle	TR230338	Kent	173
Great Addington	...	SP960750	Northants	134
Ilam	Musden Low	SK118500	Staf	111
Kesgrave	...	TM220460	Suffolk	137
Lode	Anglesey Abbey	TL530622	Cambs	135
Loudwater	...	SU900900	Bucks	159
Loughborough	...	SK535195	Leic	121
Manchester	Red Bank, Victoria Station	SJ840990	Lancs	101
Mepal	Mepal Fen	TL430820	Cambs	135
Milton	Aplin's sand pit	SP731552	Northants	146
Moggerhanger	...	TL184910	Beds	147
Netherfield	...	SK623410	Notts	112
Newtimber	Summer Down	TQ270111	Sussex	182
Orford	Charre Estate	TQ535599	Kent	171
Pagham	Churchyard	SZ883974	Sussex	182
Ribchester	...	SD650350	Lancs	95
Shiplake	...	SU775795	Oxon	159
Snettisham	...	TF683344	Norfolk	124
Somersham	...	TL360778	Hunts	135
South Moulsecoomb	Hodshrove	TQ329069	Sussex	182
Watlington	Stow Bridge	TF614070	Norfolk	124
Yarm	...	NZ418128	Yorks	85

SHIP AND BOAT BURIALS (*Possibly Christian)

Parish	Distinctive Name	Grid Reference	County	One-inch Sheet No.
Snape	...	TM402593	Suffolk	137
*Sutton (2)	Sutton Hoo	TM287487	Suffolk	150

INHUMATION BURIALS UP TO THREE IN NUMBER—(Continued)

Parish	Distinctive Name	Grid Reference	County	One-inch Sheet No.
Sowerby	Pudding Pie Hill	SE436810	Yorks	91
Sparsholt	...	SU348883	Berks	158
Spaunton	...	SE724899	Yorks	92
Spelsbury	...	SP351218	Oxon	145
Stamford Bridge	Burton Fields	SE7355	Yorks	98
Stanmer	Rocky Clump, Stanmer Park	TQ328101	Sussex	182
Stanton	Stanton Chair Roman villa	TL955742	Suffolk	136
Stanton Fitzwarren	...	SU188905	Wilts	157
Stockton	...	TM380940	Norfolk	137
Stoke Bruerne	...	SP740490	Northants	146
Stow on the Wold	...	SP191258	Glos	144
Stratton	...	SP012038	Glos	157
Streatley	...	SU592812	Berks	158
Stretton	...	SK253263	Staf	120
Stretton on the Fosse	...	SP220381	Warw	144
Strood	Railway	TQ720672	Kent	172
Strood	...	TQ729691	Kent	172
Strood	Strood Hill	TQ730693	Kent	172
Summertown	...	SP510090	Oxon	158
Sundon	Cement Works	TL037275	Beds	147
Sutton Courtenay	...	SU503937	Berks	158
Sutton in the Isle	...	TL420780	Cambs	135
Sutton Scotney	Chalk Dell	SU462391	Hants	168
Swindon	Evelyn Street	SU158832	Wilts	157
Swine	...	TA143438	Yorks	99
Sydenham	...	SP730010	Oxon	159
Tadmarton	...	SP393378	Oxon	145
Thetford	Thetford Warren	TL830830	Norfolk	136
Thorpe by Norwich	...	TG254087	Norfolk	126
Throwley	Belmont Park	TQ985564	Kent	172
Tichborne	...	SU589313	Hants	168
Tugby	Keythorpe Hall	SK767002	Leic	122
Turveston	...	SP600370	Northants	145
Twickenham	...	TQ160740	Midd	170
Twineham	Hickstead Place	TQ268199	Sussex	182
Twyford	...	SK720100	Leic	122
Uffington	...	SU310890	Berks	158
Undley	...	TL6981	Suffolk	135
Upton	...	SU514866	Berks	158
Ventnor	St. Lawrence	SZ537765	Hants	180
Wallington	Alcester Road	TQ290640	Surrey	170
Wallington	Callas Hill	SU287645	Surrey	170
Wanborough	...	SU215830	Wilts	157
Wangford	...	TL750831	Suffolk	136
Wass	Hambleton Moor	SE552807	Yorks	92
Weekley	...	SP880800	Northants	133
Welbourn	Ermine Street	SK980540	Linc	113
Wendens Ambo	Myrtle Hill	TL529363	Essex	148
Westwell	...	TQ990474	Kent	172
Wheathampstead	...	TL170140	Herts	160
Whitchurch	...	SU622781	Oxon	158
Whitlesey	Lattersey Field	TL275973	Cambs	135

LONG CIST CEMETERIES IN SCOTLAND

Parish	Distinctive Name	Grid Reference	County	One-inch Sheet No.
Abercorn	Hopetoun	NT100789	W. Lothian	61
Aberdour	Golf course	NT188846	Fife	55
Aberlemno	Flemington	NO526557	Angus	50
Arbroath	West Grange of Conon	NO573450	Angus	50
Athelstaneford	East Fortune	NT550793	E. Lothian	63
Barvas	Galson	NB440595	Lewis	8
Birsay and Harray	Brough of Birsay	HY239285	Orkney	6
Bo'ness		NS084810	W. Lothian	61
Borthwick	Arniston	NT326595	Midloth	62
Burntisland	Kingswood	NT250865	Fife	56
Carlungie, *see* Monikie				
Cockburnspath	Hoprig	NT759709	Berwick	63
Corstorphine	Gogar	NT161720	Midloth	62
Crail	Kilminning	NO61086	Fife	56
Crail	Old Haaks	NO61013	Fife	62
Currie	Harelaw	NT179657	Midloth	62
Dalkeith	New Farm	NT347688	Midloth	62
Dalmeny	Cramond Bridge	NT178754	W. Lothian	62
Dalmeny	Craigie	NT156761	W. Lothian	62
Dryden Mains, *see* Roslin				
Dumfries	Trohoughton	NX996726	Dumfrie	74
Dunbar	Kirkhill Braes	NT680790	E. Lothian	63
Dunbar	Belhaven	NT663789	E. Lothian	63
Dundee	Stannergate, Craigie	NO427310	Angus	50
East Fortune, *see* Athelstaneford				
Ecclesmachan	Burnhouse	NT039714	W. Lothian	61
Edgebucklin Brae, *see* Inveresk				
Eileach an Naoimh, *see* Jura				
Gairloch	Strath Bay	NG800771	Ross & Crom	19
Galson, *see* Barvas				
Glencorse		NT245630	Midloth	62
Gogar, *see* Corstorphine				
Haddington	Lennoxlove	NT510720	E. Lothian	63
Haddington	Camptoun	NT503778	E. Lothian	63
Harelaw, *see* Currie				
Hoprig, *see* Cockburnspath				
Humbie	Windymains	NT429641	E. Lothian	62
Inverchaolin	Ardyne	NS100860	Argyll	59
Inveresk	Edgebucklin Brae	NT358725	Midloth	62
Jedburgh	Abbey Green	NT651204	Roxb	70
Jura	Eileach an Naoimh	NM640097	Argyll	51
Kilmartin		NR828964	Argyll	52
Kingsbarns	Pitmilly Law	NO576136	Fife	56
Kirkden	Pitmuies	NO576489	Angus	50
Kirkliston	Cat Stane	NT149743	Midloth	62
Kirkliston	Hopetoun Oil Works	NT082739	W. Lothian	61
Kirkmaiden	Terally Bay	NX122412	Wigtown	79
Largo	Lundin	NO405023	Fife	56
Lasswade	Parkburn	NT298672	Midloth	62
Lauder	Addinston	NT518520	Berwick	62
Lennoxlove, *see* Haddington				
Leuchars		NO453413	Fife	56
Longforgan	Kingoodie	NO341294	Perth	50
Longniddry		NT440760	E. Lothian	62
Monikie	Carlungie	NO514362	Angus	50
Newburgh	Mare's Craig Quarry	NO247178	Fife	55
Oldhamstocks	Dunglass (Springfield)	NT751711	E. Lothian	63
Panbride	Carnoustie	NO559345	Angus	50
Pencaitland	Milton	NT453669	E. Lothian	62
Penicuik		NT230600	Midloth	62
Penicuik	North Esk Reservoir	NT155582	Midloth	62
Perth	General Railway Station	NO112232	Perth	55
Prestonpans	Cockenzie	NT400750	E. Lothian	62
Prestonpans		NT381741	E. Lothian	62
Roslin	Dryden Mains	NT278637	Midloth	62
St. Andrews	Kirkheugh	NO515166	Fife	56
Stenton	Woodend	NT619726	E. Lothian	63
Temple	Gladhouse Reservoir	NT300530	Midloth	62
Tweedsmuir	Polmood	NT111271	Peebles	69
Uphall	Wyndford	NT060732	W. Lothian	61
West Grange of Conon, *see* Arbroath				
Westruther	Hartlaw	NT646485	Berwick	63
Whitekirk	Knowes	NT610777	E. Lothian	63
Whittinghame	Nunraw	NT589707	E. Lothian	63
Whittinghame	Luggate	NT597746	E. Lothian	63
Yarrow	Yarrow Kirk	NT354277	Selk	69

SUB-ROMAN CEMETERIES

Parish	Distinctive Name	Grid Reference	County	One-inch Sheet No.
Banwell	Wint Hill	ST397584	Somerset	165
Brean	Brean Down	ST296587	Somerset	165
Camerton		ST686566	Somerset	166
Cannington	Cannington Park	ST255405	Somerset	165
Henbury	Blaise Castle	ST558784	Glos	156
Llantwit Major	Roman villa	SS959700	Glam	154
Yatton	Henley Wood	ST443652	Somerset	165

VILLAGES AND HUTS (Archaeological evidence)

Parish	Distinctive Name	Grid Reference	County	One-inch Sheet No.
Ashbocking		TM175551	Suffolk	150
Bealings, *see* Little Bealings				
Bourton on the Water	Slaughter Bridge	SP171221	Glos	144
Brandon	Staunch Meadow	TL785865	Suffolk	136
Brewer's Grave, *see* Woolsthorpe				
Brigstock		SP945855	Northants	133
Buckden		TL202680	Hunts	134
Burton upon Stather		SE896165	Linc	104
Butley	Big Mount Field, Neutral Farm	TM379500	Suffolk	150
Butley	south of Butley Church	TM374500	Suffolk	150
Caister on Sea		TG515123	Norfolk	126
Cambridge	Castle Hill	TL445592	Cambs	135
Cambridge	Market Place area	TL448583	Cambs	135
Car Dyke, *see* Waterbeach				
Cassington	Tolley's gravel pit	SP453103	Oxon	145

Parish	Distinctive Name	Grid Reference	County	One-inch Sheet No.
VILLAGES AND HUTS—(Continued)				
Cassington ...	Purwell Farm ...	SP444121 ...	Oxon ...	145
Caythorpe ...	...	SK940470 ...	Linc ...	113
Chilbolton ...	Chilbolton Common	SU389391 ...	Hants ...	168
Dorchester ...	...	SU575945 ...	Oxon ...	158
Elmswell ...	...	TA000576 ...	Yorks ...	92
Erringham, see Old Shoreham				
Eynsham ...	north of Newland Street	SP436098 ...	Oxon ...	158
Farnham ...	Firgrove Pit	SU840460 ...	Surrey ...	169
Felmersham ...	...	SP990578 ...	Beds ...	134
Grimstone End, see Pakenham				
Harrold ...	...	SP954572 ...	Beds ...	133
Harston ...	...	SK850314 ...	Leic ...	122
Hemingford Grey ...	Galley Hill	TL302690 ...	Hunts ...	134
Hensby ...	...	TL494171 ...	Norfolk ...	126
Houghton ...	...	TL287717 ...	Hunts ...	134
Houghton Regis ...	Puddle Hill	TL006235 ...	Beds ...	147
Kingston upon Thames	...	TQ185705 ...	Surrey ...	170
Linford, see Mucking				
Little Bealings ...	...	TM228464 ...	Suffolk ...	150
Manton ...	Manton Warren ...	SE930040 ...	Linc ...	104
Maxey ...	...	TF124081 ...	Northants ...	123
Medmerry, see Selsey				
Mucking ...	Linford ...	TQ672803 ...	Essex ...	171
New Fletton, see Peterborough				
Northolt ...	Northolt Manor ...	TQ132840 ...	Midd ...	160
Old Shoreham ...	Erringham ...	TQ204076 ...	Sussex ...	182
Old Windsor ...	...	SU991746 ...	Berks ...	170
Orton Longueville ...	...	TL170965 ...	Hunts ...	134
Orton Waterville ...	...	TL157963 ...	Hunts ...	134
Pakenham ...	Grimstone End ...	TL936693 ...	Suffolk ...	136
Peterborough ...	New Fletton ...	TL189974 ...	Northants ...	134
Postwick ...	...	TG300074 ...	Norfolk ...	126
Radley ...	...	SU513982 ...	Berks ...	158
Rickinghall ...	...	TM042739 ...	Suffolk ...	136
Rickinghall Superior ...	...	TM044756 ...	Suffolk ...	136
St. Neots ...	...	TL188602 ...	Hunts ...	134
Salmonby ...	Sandy Knobbs and New England	TF330734 ...	Linc ...	114
Sandrun, see West Hythe				
Seamer ...	Crossgates gravel pit	TA032832 ...	Yorks ...	93
Sedgeford ...	...	TF711363 ...	Norfolk ...	124
Selsey ...	Medmerry ...	SZ837937 ...	Sussex ...	182
Slaughter Bridge, see Bourton on the Water				
Snettisham ...	...	TF692332 ...	Norfolk ...	124
Spelsbury ...	...	SP339213 ...	Oxon ...	145
Standlake ...	...	SP385045 ...	Oxon ...	158
Staxton, see Willerby				
Sutton Courtenay ...	...	SU489940 ...	Berks ...	158
Ufton Nervet ...	...	SU617690 ...	Berks ...	158
Waterbeach ...	Car Dyke	TL489656 ...	Cambs ...	135
Wattisfield ...	...	TM006741 ...	Suffolk ...	141
West Hythe ...	Sandtun ...	TR120340 ...	Kent ...	173

Parish	Distinctive Name	Grid Reference	County	One-inch Sheet No.
West Stow ...	...	TL797714 ...	Suffolk ...	136
Willerby ...	Spital House, Staxton	TA024793 ...	Yorks ...	93
Willoughton ...	...	SK933925 ...	Linc ...	104
Windsor, see Old Windsor				
Witton ...	...	TG336320 ...	Norfolk ...	126
Woodston ...	...	TL180975 ...	Hunts ...	134
Woolsthorpe ...	Brewer's Grave ...	SK848335 ...	Linc ...	122
Worlington ...	...	TL673742 ...	Suffolk ...	135
Wykeham ...	...	SE966837 ...	Yorks ...	93
Yelford ...	...	SP360040 ...	Oxon ...	158
ROYAL AND NOBLE RESIDENCES (Archaeological evidence)				
Castle Dore, see St. Sampson				
Cheddar ...	...	ST457531 ...	Somerset...	165
Dinas Powys, see Michaelston le Pit				
Michaelston le Pit	Dinas Powys	ST149721 ...	Glam ...	154
Milfield ...	...	NT941339 ...	Northum ...	71
Old Windsor ...	...	SU991746 ...	Berks ...	170
St. Sampson ...	Castle Dore	SX103548 ...	Cornwall...	186
Yeavering ...	...	NT925305 ...	Northum ...	71
FORTIFIED SITES				
Abdie ...	Clatchard Craig	NO243178 ...	Fife ...	55
Altclut, see Dumbarton				
Anwoth ...	Trusty's Hill	NX589561 ...	Kirkcud ...	80
Arx Decantorum, see Deganwy				
Bamburgh ...	Bebbanburg ...	NU184331 ...	Northum ...	71
Beddgelert ...	Dinas Emrys ...	SH606492 ...	Caern ...	107
Carreg y Llam, see Pistyll				
Cissbury Ring, see Findon				
Clatchard Craig, see Abdie				
Coldingham ...	Coludesburh ...	NT914693 ...	Berwick ...	64
Comrie ...	Dundurn ...	NN707233 ...	Perth ...	54
Craig Phadrig, see Inverness				
Cronk Shumark, see Lezayre				
Deganwy ...	Arx Decantorum ...	SH781795 ...	Denbigh...	107
Dinas Emrys, see Beddgelert				
Din Eidyn, see Edinburgh				
Dumbarton ...	Altclut ...	NS400744 ...	Dunbar ...	60
Dunadd, see Kilmichael Glassary				
Dunaverty, see Southend				
Dunbar ...	Dynbaer ...	NT680792 ...	E. Lothian...	63
Dundurn, see Comrie				
Dunnottar ...	...Dun Fother	NO882839 ...	Kincar ...	43
Dunollie, see Kilmore				
Edinburgh ...	Din Eidyn ...	NT252735 ...	Midloth ...	62
Findon ...	Cissbury Ring	TQ140080 ...	Sussex ...	182
Hamsterley ...	The Castles	NZ103331 ...	Durham ...	84
Inverness ...	Craig Phadrig	NH640453 ...	Inver ...	28
Kilmichael Glassary	Dunadd ...	NR837936 ...	Argyll ...	52
Kilmore ...	Dunollie ...	NM852315 ...	Argyll ...	46

FORTIFIED SITES—(Continued)

Parish	Distinctive Name	Grid Reference	County	One-inch Sheet No.
Lezayre	Cronk Shumark	SC392941	I. of M.	87
Malew	South Barrule	SC257759	I. of M.	87
Pistyll	Carreg y Llam	SH334436	Caern	115
Richmond	Whitcliffe Scar	NZ135020	Yorks	91
South Barrule, see Malew				
Southend	Dunaverty	NR688074	Argyll	65
Trusty's Hill, see Anwoth				
Tynron	Tynron Doon	NX819940	Dumfrie	74
Whitcliffe Scar, see Richmond				

MEMORIAL STONES (5th and 6th Centuries) (†Ogam inscription)

The figures shown thus (41) in the second column are those given to the monuments by Nash Williams.

Parish	Distinctive Name	Grid Reference	County	One-inch Sheet No.
Abercar	(41)	SO010130	Breck	141
Abercar	(40)	SO010130	Breck	141
Aberdaron	Capel Anelog (78)	SH154278	Caern	115
Aberdaron	Gors (77)	SH154278	Caern	115
Abergwili	Pant Deuddwr (136)	SN468221	Carm	152
†Arbory (2)	Friary, Castle Rushen	SC249703	I. of M.	87
Ardoch	Greenloaning	NN831077	Perth	54
†Ballaqueeney (2)	Rushen	SC206685	I. of M.	87
Barmouth	Ceilwart Isa Farm (272)	SH604171	Meri	116
Barmouth	Sea wall (271)	SH605160	Meri	116
Bodafon	Tyddyn Holand (83)	SH793803	Caern	107
†Bodmin	Lancarffe Farm (296)	SX082690	Cornwall	185
†Brawdy (2)	Cas Wilia (298)	SM85240	Pemb	138
Brawdy	Brawdy Farm (297)	SM850240	Pemb	138
†Bridell	Rickardston Hall Farm (299)	SN176420	Pemb	139
†Brynkir	Llystyngwyn Farm (84)	SH482455	Caern	115
†Buckland Monachorum	Churchyard (300)	SX490693	Devon	187
Caerwys	Plas yn Rhos (184)	SJ117742	Flint	108
†Caldey Island	The Priory (301)	SS141962	Pemb	152
Cantref	Nant Crew Farm	SN993163	Breck	141
Cardinham	Welltown	SX136676	Cornwall	186
Cardinham	Tawna	SX134674	Cornwall	186
Cardinham		SX123687	Cornwall	186
†Castell Dwyran	Churchyard (138)	SN144182	Carm	152
Castleton	Liddisdale	NY493890	Roxb	76
Cat Stane, see Kirkliston				
Chesterholm, see Henshaw				
†Cilgerran	Churchyard (305)	SN190430	Pemb	139
†Clocaenog	Bryn y Beddau (176)	SJ052532	Denb	108
†Clydai (2)	Church (306,307)	SN250354	Pemb	139
†Clydai	Churchyard (308)	SN250354	Pemb	139
†Cornwood	Fardell Manor House	SX611574	Devon	187
†Crai	Pentre Goch Garreg (42)	SN877235	Breck	140
†Crickhowell	Ty-yn-y-wlad Farm (43)	SO225193	Breck	141
Cubert	Church	SW786577	Cornwall	185
Cuby	Tregoney Stone	SW927453	Cornwall	190
Cynwyl Gaeo (Caio)	Church (141)	SN675399	Carm	140
Cynwyl Gaeo (Caio) (2)	Maes Llanwrthwl (139, 140)	SN654371	Carm	140
†Eglwys Cymyn	Churchyard (142)	SN230106	Carm	152
Egremont	Church (143)	SN093203	Carm	139
†Fetteresso	Auquhollie Farm	NO823908	Kincar	40
Ffestiniog	Beddau Gwyr Ardudwy (277)	SH723427	Meri	116
†Gigha and Cara	Cnoc na Carraigh	NR0448	Argyll	58
Gulval	Bleu Bridge	SW478318	Cornwall	189
Gwytherin	Churchyard (177)	SH886614	Denb	108
†Henllan Amgoed	Parc y Maen (144)	SN177198	Carm	139
Henshaw	Chesterholm	NY775665	Northum	77
†Jordanston	Llangwarren Estate (312)	SM929314	Pemb	138
†Kenfig	near Pyle Station (198)	SS803847	Glam	153
†Kilmartin		NR828964	Argyll	52
†Kirk Andreas	Knoc y Doonee	NX404021	I. of M.	87
Kirkliston	Cat Stane	NT148743	Midloth	62
Kirkmadrine, see Stoneykirk				
Kirk Maughold		SC493916	I. of M.	87
Langholm	Churchyard	NY352879	Dumfrie	76
Lanivet	Churchyard	SX039642	Cornwall	185
†Lewannick	Church	SX276807	Cornwall	186
†Lewannick	Churchyard	SX276807	Cornwall	186
†Llanaelhaiarn (2)	Churchyard (86, 87)	SH387448	Caern	115
†Llanarth	Churchyard (110)	SN423177	Card	139
†Llanbabo	Llanol (6)	SH377882	Anglesey	106
†Llanboidy (2)	Church (148, 149)	SN216232	Carm	139
†Llandanwg (2)	Church (278, 279)	SH568282	Meri	116
†Llandawke	Churchyard (150)	SN282112	Carm	152
†Llanddetty	Cwm Criban (67a)	SO070120	Breck	141
Llanddewi-brefi (2)	Church (115, 116)	SN665553	Card	140
Llandefaelog-fach	Church	SO034323	Breck	141
Llandegai	Llech yr Gwyr	SH581712	Caern	107
†Llandeilo (2)	Churchyard (313, 314)	SN099269	Pemb	139
Llandeilo	Churchyard (153)	SN629222	Carm	140
†Llandysilio West (3)	Church (315, 316, 317)	SN119218	Pemb	139
†Llandysul	Churchyard (294)	SN418404	Card	139
†Llanerfyl	(10)	SJ034097	Mont	117
†Llanfaelog	Bodfeddan Farm (9)	SH350740	Anglesey	106
†Llanfaglan	Church (89)	SH476600	Caern	115
†Llanfihangel Cwm Ddu	Church (26)	SO180238	Breck	141
†Llanfihangel Cwm Ddu	1 mile S.S.W. of Church (54) east of Bwlch	SO151219	Breck	141
†Llanfihangel Ioreth	Churchyard (157)	SN456399	Carm	117
Llanfor	Church (282)	SH938367	Meri	117
Llanfyrnach	Church (320)	SN220311	Pemb	139
†Llanfyrnach	Mynydd Stamber (319)	SN190285	Pemb	139
†Llangadwaladr	Church (13)	SH385692	Anglesey	106
Llangan	N.E. of Church (322)	SN177187	Pemb	139
Llangefni	Capel Heolyn (25)	SH450777	Anglesey	106
Llangefni	Church (26)	SH458759	Anglesey	106
†Llangeler	Capel Mair (160)	SN403380	Carm	139
Llangian	Churchyard (92)	SH295289	Caern	115
Llangwyryfon	Maesllyn Farm (122)	SN588713	Card	127
Llaniltern	Church (214)	ST095799	Glam	154

MEMORIAL STONES—(Continued)

Parish	Distinctive Name	Grid Reference	County	One-inch Sheet No.
		SS438934	Glam	152
Llanmadoc	Church (215)	SH348396	Caern	115
Llannor (3)	Pempris Farm, Beudy'r Mynydd (94, 96, 97)	SH354372	Caern	115
Llannor	Churchyard (95)	SH553758	Anglesey	106
Llansadwrn	Churchyard (32)	SN281102	Carm	152
Llansadyrnin	Church (166)	SH363825	Anglesey	106
Llantrisant	Chwaen Wen House (34)	SH450809	Anglesey	106
Llantrisant	Capel Bronwen (33)	SH877315	Meri	116
Llanuwchllyn	Caer Gai (283)	SO306299	Here	142
Llanveynoe	Olchon House (409)	SN261265	Carm	139
†Llanwinio	Church (169)	SM991345	Pemb	138
Llanychaer	Church (335)	SH903190	Meri	117
Llanymawddwy	Churchyard (284)	SS563979	Glam	153
†Loughor	(228)	SS132442	Devon	163
Lundy Island	St. Helen's Chapel	SX784812	Devon	163
Lustleigh	Church	SS712490	Devon	175
Lynton		SW427353	Cornwall	189
Madron	Gun Men Scryfa Down	SN906277	Pemb	139
Maenclochog	Bwlch y Clawdd (345)	SH706386	Meri	116
Maentwrog	Tomen y Mur (285)	SN923279	Breck	141
†Maescar	Defynnog Church (44)	SN925279	Breck	141
Maescar	Capel y Fynwent	NT194307	Peebles	68
Manor	St. Gordian's	SS830887	Glam	153
†Margam	Margam Mountain (229)	SM879320	Pemb	138
Mathry	Church	SW706248	Cornwall	190
Mawgan in Meneage		SN128355	Pemb	139
Meline	Rhos Dywyrch (349)	SN352208	Carm	139
Merthyr	Churchyard (170)	SS882775	Glam	154
Merthyr Mawr	Church (238)	SX109857	Cornwall	186
†Minster	Slaughter Bridge, Worthyvale (66)	SO002150	Breck	141
Nant-ddu		SN104140	Pemb	152
Narberth North	St. Owen's Well (352)	SN083400	Pemb	139
†Nevern (2)	Church (353, 354)	SN394240	Carm	139
Newchurch	Garn Fawr (172)	SN383242	Carm	139
Newchurch	(171)	SN289513	Card	139
Penbryn	Church (126)	SH789505	Caern	116
Penmachno (4)	(101, 102, 103, 104)	SH540417	Caern	116
Penmorfa	Gesail Gyfarch Farm (105)	SH480859	Anglesey	106
Penrhoslligwy	Churchyard (39)	SH859512	Denb	107
Pentrefoelas	Doltrebeddw (183)	SW770520	Cornwall	190
Perranzabuloe	St. Piran's Oratory	SW565384	Cornwall	189
Phillack (2)	Church	SS783877	Glam	153
Port Talbot	(258)	SN008297	Pemb	151
Puncheston	Church (369)	NJ034545	Moray	29
Rafford	Altyre House	SN487428	Card	140
†Rhuddlan	Capel Wyl (127)	NY100670	Dumfrie	75
Ruthwell		SW969708	Cornwall	190
St. Breock	Nanscow	SW851439	Cornwall	185
†St. Clements	Indian Queen	SW916587	Cornwall	185
St. Columb Major	Churchyard	SW913637	Cornwall	185
St. Columb Minor	Rialton	SW856619	Cornwall	185

Parish	Distinctive Name	Grid Reference	County	One-inch Sheet No.
St. Davids	Carnhedryn Uchaf (370)	SM799280	Pemb	151
†St. Dogmells	Abbey ruins (384)	SN164459	Pemb	139
†St. Dogmells	Little Trefgarne (390)	SN164459	Pemb	139
†St. Endellion		SW989797	Cornwall	185
St. Erth	Carnsew	SW557372	Cornwall	189
St. Hilary	Church	SW559313	Cornwall	189
St. Ishmael's (2)	Church (174, 175)	SN384080	Carm	152
St. Just in Penwith	Church	SW372315	Cornwall	189
St. Just in Penwith	St. Helen's (Parken) Chapel	SW355319	Cornwall	189
†St. Kew	Church	SX021768	Cornwall	185
St. Nicholas	Churchyard (401)	SM900356	Pemb	138
St. Nicholas (2)	Llandrudian Farm (399, 400)	SM900356	Pemb	138
St. Sampson	"Tristan" Stone	SX110542	Cornwall	186
Sancreed	Churchyard	SW421294	Cornwall	189
Santon		SC330715	I. of M.	87
Scethrog	(68)	SO110248	Breck	141
Seven Sisters (Higher Neath)	Panwen Brydhin (268)	SN862096	Glam	153
†Silchester		SU640625	Hants	168
Silian	Church (128)	SN571512	Card	140
Sourton		SX547917	Devon	175
Southill	Rectory	SX329726	Cornwall	186
Spittal	Churchyard (402)	SM975229	Pemb	138
Stackpole Elidyr	Church (403)	SR987973	Pemb	151
†Steynton	Churchyard (404)	SM917078	Pemb	151
Stoneykirk (3)	Kirkmadrine	NX080483	Wigtown	79
Stowford	Churchyard	SX433870	Devon	174
Talybont	(69)	SO113226	Breck	141
Tavistock	Vicarage	SX481743	Devon	187
Tavistock	Abbey site	SX481742	Devon	187
†Tirpbil	Capel Brithdir (270)	SO137026	Glam	154
Totnes	Bowden	SX801588	Devon	188
Towyn	Churchyard (286)	SH588009	Meri	127
†Trallong	Church (70)	SN966295	Breck	141
Trawsfynydd	Rhiw Goch (289)	SH732313	Meri	116
Trawsfynydd	Bryn Goleu	SH714350	Meri	116
†Trecastle	Pentre Poeth Farm (71)	SN880290	Breck	141
†Treflys	Churchyard (106)	SH534378	Caern	116
Tregaron	Church (132)	SN680596	Card	140
Tresco	Tresco Abbey	SV891143	I. of Scilly	189
Wareham (4)	Lady St. Mary Church	SY923876	Dorset	179
Whithorn (2)		NX443392	Wigtown	80
Winsford		SS890336	Somerset	164
Yarrow	Annan Street	NT348274	Selk	69
Yealmpton	Church	SX577517	Devon	187
†Ystradfellte	Caer Madoc (74)	SN918157	Breck	141
†Ystradfellte	Maen Llia	SN924191	Breck	141
Ystradfellte	Maen Madoc (73)	SN918157	Breck	141
Ystradgynlais (2)	Church (75, 76)	SN787100	Breck	141

MONASTIC SITES

Parish	Distinctive Name	Grid Reference	County	One-inch Sheet No.
Abercorn	Aebbercurnig	NT081791	W. Lothian	62

MONASTIC SITES—(Continued)

Parish	Distinctive Name	Grid Reference	County	One-inch Sheet No.
Aberdaron	...	SH174264	Caern	115
Aberdour	Dundarg	NJ895648	Aber	31
Aberfoyle	...	NN524008	Perth	54
Abergele	Opergelei	SH946774	Denb	108
Abingdon	Abbandun	SU491971	Berks	158
Ailech, Insula, see Jura				
All Hallows, Barking	...	TQ335806	London	160
Annait, see Duirinish				
Applecross	Aporcrosan	NG713445	Ross & Crom	25
Bangor	Bancor	SH580720	Caern	106
Bangor	Bancornaburg	SJ386454	Flintshire	109
Banwell	...	ST399592	Somerset	165
Bardney	Beardaneu	TF119692	Linc	113
Bardsey	Enli	SH120222	Caern	115
Barking	(in) Berecingum	TQ450840	Essex	161
Barrow upon Humber	(ad) Baruae	TA072215	Linc	99
Bath	Bathanceaster	ST750650	Somerset	156
Beckford	Beccanford	SO975358	Worc	144
Bellimoor, see Preston on Wye				
Berkeley	Berclea	ST684993	Glos	156
Bermondsey	Vermundesei	TQ340790	London	170
Beverley	Inderawood	TA031399	Yorks	99
Birsay and Harray	Birsay	HY239285	Orkney	7
Bishopston	Llandeilo Ferwallt	SS578893	Glam	153
Bishop's Waltham	Waldheim	SU556176	Hants	180
Bodmin	Dinurrin	SX073670	Cornwall	185
Bosham	Bosanhamm	SU804039	Sussex	181
Bradford on Avon	Bradanford	ST824609	Wilts	166
Bradwell on Sea	Ythancaestir	TM031082	Essex	162
Breedon on the Hill	Briudun	SK405234	Leic	121
Brixworth	...	SP747712	Northants	133
Bromyard	Bromgeard	SO655548	Worc	142
Buchanan	Strathcashell Point	NS393931	Stirl	53
Buchanan	Knock in Haglish	NS487849	Stirl	53
Burgh Castle	Cnobheresburg	TG475046	Suffolk	126
Burrian, see Cross and Burness				
Bury St. Edmunds	Beadricesworth	TL858641	Suffolk	136
Caer Gybi, see Holyhead				
Cambuslang	...	NS636600	Lanark	60
Canna	Sgur nam Ban-naomha	NG230042	Inner Heb	33
Canterbury	St. Augustine's	TR155579	Kent	173
Carlisle	Luel	NY399559	Cumb	76
Castor	...	TL125985	Northants	134
Cerne Abbas	...	ST665015	Dorset	178
Cheltenham	Celtanhom	SO950220	Glos	144
Chertsey	Cerotaesi	TQ046470	Surrey	170
Clife at Hoo	...	TQ736766	Kent	171
Clynnog Fawr	...	SH415499	Caern	115
Coldingham	Coludesburh	NT910680	Berwick	64
Congresbury	...	ST435637	Somerset	165
Cookham	Coccham	SU898855	Berks	159
Coquet Island	Cocwaedsae	NU294046	Northum	71

Parish	Distinctive Name	Grid Reference	County	One-inch Sheet No.
Corbridge	Corabrig	NY988645	Northum	77
Coventry	...	SP335790	Warw	132
Crayke	...	SE560707	Yorks	92
Crediton	Cridiantun	SS836001	Devon	176
Cross and Burness	Burrian, North Ronaldsay	HY763514	Orkney	5
Crowland	Cruglond	TF250109	Linc	123
Dacor	Dacor	NY461265	Cumb	83
Dacre, see Old Deer				
Deerhurst	St. Mary	SO870299	Glos	143
Deerness	Brough of Deerness	HY596088	Orkney	6
Dorchester	Dorcic	SU579942	Oxon	158
Dover	Dofras	TR320415	Kent	173
Duirinish	Annait	NG272328	Inner Heb	24
Dunblane	...	NN782015	Perth	54
Dunrossness	St. Ninian's Isle	HU366206	Zetland	4
Eastry	...	TR312548	Kent	172
Ebchester	...	NZ100554	Durham	78
Ely	Elge	TL541802	Camb	135
Evesham	Cronuchomme	SP033434	Worc	144
Exeter	(ad) Escancastre	SX921925	Devon	176
Farne Islands	...	NU220360	Northum	71
Fearn	Nova Ferna	NH837773	Ross & Crom	22
Felixstowe	Dommoc	TM123358	Suffolk	150
Ferring	...	TQ094026	Sussex	182
Fladbury	Flaedanburh	SO996463	Worc	143
Folkestone	Folcanstan	TR230363	Kent	173
Frome	Frocom	ST777479	Somerset	166
Gainford	...	NZ169167	Durham	85
Garway	Llan Gurboe	SO455224	Here	142
Gateshead	Ad Caprae Caput	NZ265630	Durham	78
Gilling West	(in) Getlingum	NZ181051	Yorks	85
Glasbury	...	SO177392	Rad	141
Glascwm	...	SO155531	Rad	141
Glasgow	...	NS563654	Lanark	60
Glastonbury	Glestingaburg	ST500388	Somerset	165
Gloucester	Gleawanceaster	SO831189	Glos	143
Hackness	Hacanos	SE969905	Yorks	93
Hanbury	...	SO961642	Worc	130
Hartlepool	Heruteu	NZ520330	Durham	85
Hereford	...	SO510398	Here	142
Hexham	Hagustaldesae	NY935641	Northum	77
Hoddom	...	NY166727	Dumfrie	75
Holyhead	Caer Gybi	SH247826	Anglesey	106
Horning	St. Benet at Hulme	TG383156	Norfolk	126
Insula Ailech, see Jura				
Iona	Ii	NM286245	Argyll	51
Ismere	Husmere	SO865796	Worc	130
Jarrow	(in) Gyruum	NZ338623	Durham	78
Jura	Insula Ailech	NM646097	Argyll	51
Kilmuir	Loch Chaluim-Chille	NG376689	Inner Heb	24
Kilnsea	Spurn Point	TA4112	Yorks	105
Kingarth	...	NS091561	Bute	59
Kinross	St. Serf's, Loch Leven	NO161003	Kinross	55
Kirkmadrine, see Stoneykirk				

MONASTIC SITES—(Continued)

Parish	Distinctive Name	Grid Reference	County	One-inch Sheet No.
Landochou, see St. Kew				
Lastingham	Laestinga Eu	SE728904	Yorks	92
Leicester		SK580050	Leic	121
Leominster		SO498592	Here	129
Lewes	South Malling	TQ415110	Sussex	183
Lichfield	Stow	SK122103	Staf	120
Lindisfarne	Metcaut	NU128418	Northum	64
Lismore		NM861435	Argyll	46
Llanartheny		SN535203	Carm	140
Llanbadarn-fawr		SN599810	Card	127
Llancarvan	Nant Carban	ST051702	Glam	154
Llandaff	Lan Tam	ST158781	Glam	154
Llanddeusant		SN775245	Carm	140
Llanddewi-brefi		SN663553	Card	140
Llandilo-fawr		SN630225	Carm	140
Llandinam		SO025886	Mont	128
Llandough		SS994729	Glam	154
Llandrillo		SH832808	Denb	107
Llangorse		SO135276	Breck	141
Llangurig		SN907799	Mont	128
Llangyfelach		SS646990	Glam	153
Llangynog	Pennant Melangell	SJ024266	Mont	117
Llanrhaiader Mochnant				
Llansilin		SJ210282	Denb	117
Llantwit Major	Lan Ildut	SS965686	Glam	154
Llanynys		SJ103627	Denb	108
Loch Chaluim-Chille, see Kilmuir				
London	St. Paul's	TQ320810	London	160
Luss		NS361928	Dunbar	53
Lyminge	Liminge	TR161409	Kent	173
Magh Lunge, see Tiree				
Malmesbury	Maldubesburg	ST933874	Wilts	157
Margam	Marcan	SS801864	Glam	153
Medeshamstede, see Peterborough				
Meifod		SJ155132	Mont	117
Melrose	Mailros	NT549342	Roxb	63
Merthyr Mawr		SS883777	Glam	154
Minster in Sheppey		TQ956730	Kent	172
Minster in Thanet	Suthmynster	TR311642	Kent	173
Moccas	Mochros	SO357428	Here	142
Much Dewchurch	Llanddewi	SO482311	Here	142
Muchelney		ST429249	Somerset	177
Much Wenlock	Wimnicas	SJ625000	Salop	129
Munkerhouse, see Papa Westray				
Nevern	Nant Nimer	SN083400	Pemb	139
Newport		ST311885	Monm	155
North Elmham		TF988216	Norfolk	125
Nursling	Nhutscelle	SU359165	Hants	180
Old Deer	Dear	NJ968481	Aber	31
Oundle	(in)Undalum	TL036880	Northants	134
Oxford	St. Frideswide's	SP315060	Oxon	158
Padstow	St. Petroc	SW920753	Cornwall	185
Papa Westray	Munkerhouse	HY488528	Orkney	5
Papil		HU368315	Zetland	4
Partney	Peartan Eu	TF410683	Linc	114
Peakirk		TF160065	Northants	123
Peel	Peel Island	SC242845	I. of M.	87
Penally	Pen Alun	SS118991	Pemb	152
Pennant Melangell, see Llangynog				
Pershore		SO948459	Worc	144
Peterborough	Medeshamstede	TL193986	Northants	134
Polesworth		SK264024	Warw	120
Preston on Wye	Bellimoor, Bolgros	SO395406	Here	142
Priestholm	Glannauc	SH652821	Anglesey	107
Reculver	Raculf	TR227694	Kent	173
Redbridge	Hreutford	SU370136	Hants	180
Repton	Hreopedun	SK302271	Derby	120
Ripon	(in) Hrypum	SE315711	Yorks	91
Rochester	Hrofescaestir	TQ740684	Kent	171
Romsey		SU351213	Hants	168
Rushen	St. Lua or St. Leoc	SC278702	I. of M.	87
Ruthwell		NY100675	Dumfrie	75
St. Albans	Uerlamacaestir	TL145071	Herts	160
St. Andrews		NO515167	Fife	56
St. Asaph	Lann Elgui	SJ037742	Flint	108
St. Benet at Hulme, see Horning				
St. Bertelin, see Stafford				
St. Davids	Menevia	SM752255	Pemb	138
St. Frideswide, see Oxford				
St. Germans		SX359178	Cornwall	186
St. Harmon		SN988728	Rad	128
St. Helens, see Tresco				
St. Kew	Landochou or Lanow	SX021779	Cornwall	186
St. Lua or Leoc, see Rushen				
St. Maughold		SC493916	I. of M.	87
St. Paul's, see London				
St. Petroc, see Padstow				
St. Serf, Loch Leven, see Kinross				
Sandbach		SJ766610	Cheshire	110
Selsey		SZ859910	Sussex	181
Sgur nam Ban-naomha, see Canna				
Sherborne	Sciraburna	ST638165	Dorset	178
Sockburn		NZ349071	Durham	85
South Elmham	All Saints	TM388826	Suffolk	137
Southill		SX329726	Cornwall	186
South Malling, see Lewes				
South Molton		SS713260	Devon	163
Spurn Point, see Kilnsea				
Stafford	St. Bertelin	SJ921232	Staf	119
Stanmer		TQ337096	Sussex	182
Stoneykirk	Kirkmadrine	NX080484	Wigtown	79
Stow, see Lichfield				
Stratford on Avon		SP201543	Warw	144
Taunton	Tantun	ST227245	Somerset	177
Tetbury		ST890930	Glos	156

SECULAR CHURCHES OF PRE-871 DATE

§ *For want of space the churches thus distinguished have not been shown on the map.*

Parish	Distinctive Name	Grid Reference	County	One-inch Sheet No.
Bardsey	All Hallows	SE366432	Yorks	96
Bishopstone	St. Andrew	TQ472010	Sussex	183
Brigstock	St. Andrew	SP946852	Northants	133
Britford	St. Peter	SU163284	Wilts	167
Bywell	St. Peter	NZ049614	Northum	77
§Canterbury	St. Martin	TR158877	Kent	173
§Canterbury	St. Mary	TR155577	Kent	173
§Canterbury	St. Pancras	TR155577	Kent	173
§Canterbury	Ss. Peter and Paul	TR155577	Kent	173
Cardross	Kirkton of Kilmahew	NS345784	Dunbar	59
Escomb	St. John	NZ189301	Durham	85
Geddington	St. Mary Magdalene	SP895830	Northants	133
Hart	St. Mary Magdalene	NZ470352	Durham	85
Heddon on the Wall	St. Andrew	NZ135669	Northum	78
Heysham	St. Patrick and St. Peter	SD416617	Lancs	89
Kirby Hill	All Saints	SE393686	Yorks	91
Kirkton of Kilmahew, *see* Cardross				
Ledsham	All Saints	SE456297	Yorks	97
§London	All Hallows by the Tower	TQ335807	Midd	160
Papa Westray	St. Tredwell	HY486509	Orkney	5
Papil, *see* West Burra				
§Rochester	St. Andrew	TQ742684	Kent	172
Seaham	St. Mary	NZ422505	Durham	78
Skipwith	St. Helen	SE657384	Yorks	97
Somerford Keynes	All Saints	SU016955	Glos	157
South Kyme		TF170498	Linc	113
Staindrop	St. Mary	NZ131206	Durham	85
Stoke d'Abernon	St. Mary	TQ129584	Surrey	170
Stone by Faversham		TQ991613	Kent	172
§Titchfield	St. Peter	SU540057	Hants	180
West Burra	St. Lawrence, Papil	HU369315	Shetland	4
Wing	All Saints	SP880225	Bucks	146
Yeavering		NT925305	Northum	71
§York	St. Mary Bishophill Senior	SE601514	Yorks	97

CHAPELS, ORATORIES AND HERMITAGES

Parish	Distinctive Name	Grid Reference	County	One-inch Sheet No.
Barvas	North Rona	HW809322	Lewis	8
Brampton	Ninewells	NY531612	Cumb	76
Brougham	St. Ninian's Church	NY560300	Westm	83
Chapel Finnian, *see* Mochrum				
Ettrick	Over Kirkhope	NT211122	Selk	69
Glasserton	St. Ninian's Cave	NX423360	Wigtown	80
Lundy	Chapel of St. Elene Regina	SS132442	Devon	163
Malham	Malham Moor	SD897674	Yorks	90
Mochrum	Chapel Finnian	NX278489	Wigtown	80
North Bute	St. Ninian's Chapel	NS035612	Bute	59
North Rona, *see* Barvas				
Over Kirkhope, *see* Ettrick				

MONASTIC SITES—(Continued)

Parish	Distinctive Name	Grid Reference	County	One-inch Sheet No.
Threckingham		TF089361	Linc	113
Tilbury	Tilaburg	TQ642763	Essex	171
Tintagel		SX093890	Cornwall	185
Tiree	Magh Lunge	NL985420	Argyll	44
Tisbury	Tyssesburg	ST944293	Wilts	167
Towyn		SH587010	Meri	127
Tynemouth	Tinamutha	NZ373694	Northum	78
Tyninghame		NT610790	E. Lothian	63
Wareham	Werham	SY923875	Dorset	178
Watton	Uetadun	TA013507	Yorks	99
Wearmouth	Uiuraemuda	NZ390570	Durham	78
Wells	Wiela	ST551459	Somerset	165
West Wittering		SZ777984	Sussex	181
Whitby	Streanaeshalch	NZ901113	Yorks	86
Whithorn	Candida Casa	NX446403	Wigtown	80
Wilton	Wiltun	SU095313	Wilts	167
Wimborne Minster	Winburna	SU009000	Dorset	178
Winchcombe		SP024282	Glos	144
Winchester	Uintancaestir	SU482292	Hants	168
Withington	Wudiandun	SP031156	Glos	144
Woking	Woccingas	TQ020569	Surrey	169
Worcester	Wigranceastre	SO810545	Worc	143
York	Eoferwic	SE603522	Yorks	97

BISHOPS' SEATS

Parish	Distinctive Name	Grid Reference	County	One-inch Sheet No.
Abercorn		NT081791	W. Lothian	62
Alba, *see* Dunkeld				
Bodmin		SX073670	Cornwall	186
Canterbury		TR151579	Kent	173
Dorchester		SU579942	Oxon	158
Dunkeld		NO027425	Perth	49
Felixstowe	Dommoc	TM323358	Suffolk	150
Glasgow		NS603655	Lanark	60
Hereford		SO510398	Here	142
Hexham		NY935641	Northum	77
Leicester		SK583049	Leic	121
Lichfield		SK116098	Staf	120
Lindisfarne		NU140415	Northum	71
London		TQ320811		160
North Elmham		TF988217	Norfolk	125
Ripon		SE314711	Yorks	91
Rochester		TQ743685	Kent	171
Selsey		SZ858925	Sussex	181
Sherborne		ST631160	Dorset	178
Whithorn		NX444404	Wigtown	80
Winchester		SU483293	Hants	168
Worcester		SO810545	Worc	143
York		SE603522	Yorks	97

CHAPELS, ORATORIES AND HERMITAGES—(Continued)

Parish	Distinctive Name	Grid Reference	County	One-inch Sheet No.
Patrick...	Lag na Keeilley ...	SC216745	I. of M. ...	87
Penmon ...	Puffin Island, Ynys Seiriol	SH629807	Anglesey...	107
Rushden ...	Calf of Man, Bushell's House ...	SC152659	I. of M. ...	87
St. Constantine's Chapel, see St. Merryn				
St. David's ...	St. Patrick's Chapel ...	SM733272	Pemb	138
St. Helen's Island, see Tresco				
St. Merryn ...	St. Constantine's Chapel ...	SW865749	Cornwall...	185
St. Ninian's Cave, see Glasserton				
St. Ninian's Chapel, Bute, see North Bute				
St. Patrick's Chapel, see St. David's				
Tean, see Tresco				
Tresco...	St. Helen's Island ...	SV900170	I. of Scilly	189
Tresco...	Tean ...	SV908165	I. of Scilly	189

MANX RHULLICKS AND KEEILLS

Parish	Distinctive Name	Grid Reference	County	One-inch Sheet No.
Andreas	Knock e Dooney ...	NX403021	I. of M. ...	87
Arbory	Ballagawne ...	SC239718	I. of M. ...	87
Arbory	Bemaken... ...	SC249703	I. of M. ...	87
Braddan	Speke ...	SC333746	I. of M. ...	87
Braddan	Keeill Abban ...	SC360822	I. of M. ...	87
Bride	Faaie Rhullick, Ballavarkish	NX459007	I. of M. ...	87
German	Keeill Pharick a droma ...	SC297868	I. of M. ...	87
German	Knocksharry ...	SC274817	I. of M. ...	87
German	Keeill Moirrey ...	SC263834	I. of M. ...	87
German	Keeill Beary ...	SC305844	I. of M. ...	87
German	Ballahowin ...	SC281817	I. of M. ...	87
Jurby	Greeba Mill ...	SC299813	I. of M. ...	87
Jurby	St. Patrick's Chapel ...	SC346680	I. of M. ...	87
Lezayre	Ballachurry ...	SC375983	I. of M. ...	87
Lezayre	Cronk yn Howe... ...	SC435996	I. of M. ...	87
Lezayre	Magher ny Hoaieghyn, Skyhill	SC426931	I. of M. ...	87
Lezayre	Bellevue... ...	SC395945	I. of M. ...	87
Lonan	Groudle, Ballaleaney ...	SC427793	I. of M. ...	87
Lonan	Keeill Vian ...	SC427845	I. of M. ...	87
Lonan	Kill Kellan ...	SC432824	I. of M. ...	87
Lonan	St. Nicholas' Chapel, Skinscoe...	SC442859	I. of M. ...	87
Lonan	Keeill Woirrey, Gretch vooar	SC436848	I. of M. ...	87
Malew	Ballakilley ...	SC284731	I. of M. ...	87
Malew	Kerrowkiel ...	SC261734	I. of M. ...	87
Malew	Knockrenny ...	SC299738	I. of M. ...	87
Malew	Rullic y doonee, Intack...	SC276771	I. of M. ...	87
Malew	Lorne House, Bowling Green, Castletown	SC267677	I. of M. ...	87
Malew	St. Mary's Chapel, Castletown...	SC265673	I. of M. ...	87
Malew	Ballabeg... ...	SC264716	I. of M. ...	87
Marown	Ballaquiney ...	SC333776	I. of M. ...	87
Marown	Ballachrink ...	SC307767	I. of M. ...	87
Marown	Church of St. Runn ...	SC321786	I. of M. ...	87
Marown	Cabbal Druiaght ...	SC314781	I. of M. ...	87
Marown	St. Trinian's ...	SC317802	I. of M. ...	87
Marown	Keeill Vreeshy, Ballaharry	SC331801	I. of M. ...	87
Maughold	Ballacorteen ...	SC460890	I. of M. ...	87
Maughold	Ballaglass ...	SC461905	I. of M. ...	87
Maughold	Rullic Keeill vael ...	SC461875	I. of M. ...	87
Maughold	Cardle veg ...	SC455901	I. of M. ...	87
Maughold	Keeill Folieu, Port y vullin	SC473929	I. of M. ...	87
Maughold	Keeill Woirrey, Corna ...	SC432894	I. of M. ...	87
Maughold	Ballagilley ...	SC454915	I. of M. ...	87
Maughold	Ard Cooillen ...	SC450872	I. of M. ...	87
Michael	Keeill Pharlane ...	SC320931	I. of M. ...	87
Michael	Cabbal Pherrick ...	SC307887	I. of M. ...	87
Michael	Cooilldarragh ...	SC318897	I. of M. ...	87
Onchan	Ballaquayle ...	SC380767	I. of M. ...	87
Onchan	Keeill Martin ...	SC495794	I. of M. ...	87
Onchan	Upper Sulby ...	SC378800	I. of M. ...	87
Patrick...	Keeill Woirrey ...	SC269790	I. of M. ...	87
Patrick...	Ballaquayle ...	SC257816	I. of M. ...	87
Patrick...	Keeill yn Chiarn ...	SC220788	I. of M. ...	87
Patrick...	Rheaby ...	SC230805	I. of M. ...	87
Rushen	The Smelt, Bay ny Carrickey	SC215687	I. of M. ...	87
Rushen	Rullic y lagg shliggah, Shenvalley	SC176667	I. of M. ...	87
Rushen	Ballaqueeney ...	SC206685	I. of M. ...	87
Rushen	The Howe, Glenchass ...	SC199677	I. of M. ...	87
Rushen	Magher y Chabbal, Bradda	SC200703	I. of M. ...	87
Santon...	Ballavale... ...	SC315724	I. of M. ...	87
Santon...	St. Ann's Church ...	SC310711	I. of M. ...	87
Santon...	Cronk ny Merriu, Arragon Veg	SC317704	I. of M. ...	87
Santon...	Ballacregga ...	SC343721	I. of M. ...	87
Santon...	Sulbrick ...	SC309746	I. of M. ...	87

MINOR CHRISTIAN MONUMENTS IN WALES (7th to 9th centuries)

The figures shown thus (137) in the second column are those given to the monuments by Nash Williams.

Parish	Distinctive Name	Grid Reference	County	One-inch Sheet No.
Abergwili	Capel y Groes (137) ...	SN444243	Carm	139
Bargoed	Capel Brithdir ...	SO139025	Glam	154
Bryngwyn	Churchyard (405) ...	SO186496	Rad	141
Capel Colman...	near Church (302) ...	SN216386	Pemb	139
Carno...	Church ...	SN957973	Mont	128
Castlemartin	Church (304) ...	SR910988	Pemb	151
Corwen	Church (273) ...	SJ078434	Meri	108
Eglwysilan	Church (195) ...	ST106890	Glam	154
Eliseg's Pillar, see Llantysilio yn Ial				
Fochriw	Cefn Gelligaer (197) ...	SO103034	Glam	154
Glan Beuno, see Waenfawr				
Henfynyw	Church (108) ...	SN447612	Card	139
Jefferston	Church (309) ...	SN089065	Pemb	151
Kenfig...	Marlas Farm (199) ...	SS821823	Glam	153
Lampeter	Pont Faen (109) ...	SN570482	Card	140
Llanaelhaiarn ...	Churchyard (115) ...	SH387448	Caern	115
Llanafan Fawr	Church (45) ...	SN069557	Breck	141
Llandanwg	Church ...	SH579310	Meri	116

MINOR CHRISTIAN MONUMENTS—(Continued)

Parish	Distinctive Name	Grid Reference	County	One-inch Sheet No.
Llanddetty	Church (46)	SO128202	Breck	141
Llanddewi-brefi (4)	Churchyard (117-120)	SN663553	Card	140
Llanddowror (2)	Churchyard (151, 152)	SN256145	Carm	152
Llandeilo	Cefn Cethin Farm (154)	SN625188	Carm	153
Llandulas	Pen-lan-wen, Tir Abad (48)	SN893418	Breck	141
Llanegryn	Church (280)	SH596057	Meri	127
Llanelieu (2)	Church (51, 52)	SO185341	Breck	141
Llanfeagan	Ty Newydd Farm (53)	SO084261	Breck	141
Llanfihangel-ar-Arth	Church (158)	SN459399	Carm	139
Llanfihangel-ystrad	Cribyn, Gaer Camp (107)	SN520508	Card	140
Llanfrynach	(55)	SO075257	Breck	141
Llanfyrnach	Rhyd-y-garth (321)	SN214312	Pemb	139
Llangamarch	Church (57)	SN934473	Breck	141
Llangamarch	Cildu Farm (58)	SN930470	Breck	141
Llangernyw (2)	Churchyard (178, 179)	SH875674	Denb	107
Llanglydwen	Churchyard (161)	SN174265	Carm	139
Llangors	Church (59)	SO135276	Breck	141
Llangunnor	Church (162)	SN430202	Carm	152
Llangwnadl, *see* Tudweilioc				
Llangwyryfon	Churchyard (123)	SN596705	Card	127
Llangybi	(93)	SH428411	Caern	115
Llangyndeirn	Closteg Farm (163)	SN453151	Carm	152
Llanllawer (2)	Churchyard (323, 324)	SM986559	Pemb	138
Llanlleonfel	Churchyard (62)	SN938499	Breck	141
Llanllwyni	Maes Nonni Farm (164)	SN497396	Carm	140
Llanllyr	Llanllyr House (124)	SN544559	Card	140
Llanmadoc (2)	Churchyard (216, 217)	SS438934	Glam	152
Llanpumpsaint	Churchyard (165)	SN418290	Carm	139
Llanreithan	Mesur-y-Dorth Farm (325)	SM838306	Pemb	138
Llansadyrnin	Parc-y-Cerrig Santaidd (167)	SN266111	Carm	152
Llansantfraid-cwmdeuddwr	Nant Gwynllyn (407)	SN943698	Rad	128
Llansawel	Church (168)	SN620362	Carm	140
Llanspyddid	Churchyard (63)	SO011281	Breck	141
Llantrisant	Church (219)	ST046834	Glam	154
Llantysilio-yn-Ial	Valle Crucis Abbey, Eliseg's Pillar (182)	SJ202445	Denb	108
Llanwnda	Llanwnwr Farm (326)	SM895405	Pemb	138
Llanwnda	Pont-yr-Eglwys (327)	SM924394	Pemb	138
Llanwnda	Cemetery cross roads (333)	SM946392	Pemb	138
Llanwnda (5)	Church (328-32)	SM932395	Pemb	138
Llanwonno	Church (227)	ST030956	Glam	154
Llanwrtyd	Llawdre Farm (64)	SN858450	Breck	140
Llanychaer	(337)	SN999349	Pemb	138
Llanychllwydog (4)	Church (336)	SM991345	Pemb	138
Llawhaden	Churchyard (338-341)	SN012343	Pemb	151
Llysfran	St. Kennox Farm (342)	SN074162	Pemb	151
Mathry	Velindre Farm (344)	SN044257	Pemb	138
Mathry	Tregidreg Farm (347)	SM869310	Pemb	138
Mathry	Rhoslanog Farm (348)	SM879319	Pemb	138
Merthyr Tydfil	Church (248)	SO048065	Glam	154
Morvil	Churchyard (350)	SN036307	Pemb	138
Mountain Ash	Panwaen Pwll Gwellt (249)	SO050015	Glam	154
Moylgrove	Penprisk Farm (351)	SN122446	Pemb	139
Nash	Nash Manor (250)	SS964728	Glam	154
Neath	Court Herbert (251)	SS744977	Glam	153
Nefyn	Ty Mawr Farm (98)	SH319418	Caern	115
Nefyn	Ty'n Cae Farm (99)	SH312410	Caern	115
Nefyn	near the Vicarage (100)	SH308404	Caern	115
Nevern (3)	(355)	SN083400	Pemb	139
	Brynberian, Tre-bwlch Farm (356-8)			
Newborough	Fron-Deg Farm (55)	SN459399	Pemb	139
Newchurch	Llanfihangel Croesfeini churchyard (173)	SH446675	Anglesey	106
Newport	near churchyard (361)	SN394440	Carm	152
Newport	Cnwc-y-Crogwydd (362)	SN058388	Pemb	138
Penally	Churchyard (363)	SS117991	Pemb	152
Penmachno	Churchyard (104a)	SH789505	Caern	107
Pontfaen (2)	Churchyard (367-8)	SN021341	Pemb	138
Pontrhydfen	Penhydd Farm (257)	SS801920	Glam	153
Port Talbot	Cwrt Isaf Farm (259)	SS765905	Glam	153
Port Talbot	Croft Farm (260)	SS760900	Glam	153
Port Talbot	(262)	SS767895	Glam	153
Resolven	Carn Caca	SN826006	Glam	153
St. Davids	Pen Arthur Farm (373)	SM748265	Pemb	138
St. Davids	St. Non's Chapel (372)	SM750243	Pemb	138
St. Davids	(371)	SM804282	Pemb	138
St. Dogmaels (2)	The Abbey (385, 387)	SN164458	Pemb	139
St. Dogmaels (2)	Church (386, 388)	SN164459	Pemb	139
St. Dogmaels (Municipal)	Bryngwyn Farm (130)	SN168451	Card	139
St. Elvies	St. Elvies Farmhouse (395)	SM812241	Pemb	138
Silian	Churchyard (129)	SN571512	Card	140
Strata Florida	Abbey Cemetery (131)	SN746657	Card	127
Towyn	(287)	SH588009	Meri	127
Tregaron (3)	Church (133-5)	SN680596	Card	140
Tudweiliog	Llangwnadl Church	SH208832	Caern	115
Vaenor	(72)	SO034089	Breck	154
Waenfawr	Glan Beuno	SH483601	Caern	115

FREE-STANDING CROSSES

Parish	Distinctive Name	Grid Reference	County	One-inch Sheet No.
Abercorn		NT081791	W. Lothian	61
Aberlady		NT461799	E. Lothian	62
Addingham		NY560380	Cumb	83
Bakewell		SK216684	Derby	111
Bewcastle		NY565746	Cumb	76
Bishop Auckland		NZ213303	Durham	85
Boroughbridge		SE395665	Yorkshire	91
Bradbourne		SK207527	Derby	111
Closeburn		NX904924	Dumfries	74
Coldingham		NT901659	Berwick	64
Collingham	St. Oswald's Church	SE390462	Yorks	96

PICTISH SYMBOL STONES (†stone has Ogam inscription)

Parish	Distinctive Name	Grid Reference	County	One-inch Sheet No.
Abdie ...	Lindores...	NO261169	Fife	56
Aberlemno ...		NO522555	Angus	50
Aberlemno ...	Flemington Farm	NO544555	Angus	50
Abernethy ...		NO188166	Perth	55
Abernethy and Kincardine	Congash Farm	NJ058262	Inver	38
†Aboyne ...	Formaston	NO570980	Aber	40
Advie ...		NJ140350	Moray	29
Aikerness, see Evie and Rendall				
Alness ...	Nonakiln kirkyard, Roskeen	NH663712	Ross & Crom	22
Alness ...	Clach a'Mheirilich	NH681690	Ross & Crom	22
Alvie ...	Dunachton	NH821048	Inver	37
Alyth ...	Bruceton...	NO290504	Perth	49
Anwoth ...	Trusty's Hill	NX589560	Kirkcud	80
Arbirlot ...		NO601406	Angus	50
Ardlair, see Kennethmont				
Arndilly, see Boharm				
Baggerton, see Forfar				
Balnellan, see Kirkmichael				
Barra ...	Pabbay	NL607875	Outer Heb	32
Benbecula ...	Stromé Shunnamal	NF800560	Outer Heb	23
Birnie ...		NJ206586	Moray	29
Birsay and Harray	Knowe of Burrian	HY324180	Orkney	6
Birsay and Harray	Brough of Birsay	HY233285	Orkney	6
Blackford ...	Peterhead Farm...	NN924097	Perth	55
Blair Atholl ...	Struan ...	NN818654	Perth	48
Boar's Stone, see Inverness and Bona				
Boharm ...	Arndilly ...	NJ284469	Banff	29
Borthwick Mains, see Roberton				
Bourtie ...		NJ804449	Aber	40
Bracadale ...	Fiscavaig, Minginish	NG330340	Inner Heb	33
Brandsbutt, see Inverurie				
Bruceton, see Alyth				
Burrian ...	Broch of Burrian (bone)	HY763514	Orkney	5
Cairnie (3) ...	Tillytarmont	NJ529464	Aber	39
Cargill ...	Whitefield Farm...	NO160345	Perth	49
Carn Greg, see Monifieth				
Ceres ...	Walton ...	NO360090	Fife	56
†Chapel of Garioch (3)	Logie Elphinstone	NJ703258	Aber	40
Clach Ard, see Snizort				
Clach Biorach, see Edderton				
Clach a'Mheirilich, see Alness				
Clach an Tiumpan, see Strathpeffer				
Clatt ...	Percylieu...	NJ535264	Aber	39
Clatt ...	Kirkyard...	NJ539260	Aber	39
Cluny ...	Nether Corskie	NJ748096	Aber	40
Clyne (2) ...	Clynekirkton	NC890406	Suther	15
Clyne (2) ...	Clynemilton	NC914069	Suther	15
Clynekirkton, see Clyne				
Clynemilton, see Clyne				
Cnoc an Fruich, see Cromdale				
Collace ...	Fairygreen	NO212328	Perth	49

FREE STANDING CROSSES—(Continued)

Parish	Distinctive Name	Grid Reference	County	One-inch Sheet No.
Colonsay ...	Riskbuie...	NM443005	Argyll	51
Croft ...	St. Peter's Church	NZ289099	Yorks	85
Cropthorne ...		SO999452	Worc	144
Dacre ...		NY461265	Cumb	83
Dewsbury ...	All Saints' Church	SE240220	Yorks	96
Easby ...		NZ185003	Yorks	91
Edenham ...		TF062218	Linc	123
Edzell ...		NO590690	Angus	50
Eilean Mor, see North Knapdale				
Eyam ...		SK217765	Derby	111
Hackness ...		SE969905	Yorks	93
Heversham ...		SD496834	Westm	89
Heysham ...		SD416617	Lancs	94
Hoddom ...		NY166727	Dumfrie	75
Hornby ...		SD585686	Lancs	89
Ilkley ...		SE116478	Yorks	96
Iona ...		NM287245	Argyll	57
Irton ...		NY091004	Cumb	88
Jedburgh ...		NT649206	Roxb	70
Keills, see North Knapdale				
Kendal ...		SD510920	Westm	89
Kilchoman ...	Kilneave...	NR286715	Argyll	57
Kildalton ...		NR438478	Argyll	57
Kilfinan ...		NR934789	Argyll	58
Kilmartin ...		NR835988	Argyll	52
Kilmory ...	Kilmory Knap	NR869867	Argyll	52
Kilneave, see Kilchoman				
Lancaster ...		SD474620	Lancs	89
Lastingham ...		SE728905	Yorks	92
Llangynog ...	Pennant Melangell	SJ024266	Mont	117
Lypiatt ...		SO886058	Glos	156
Masham ...		SE226806	Yorks	91
Morham ...		NT556726	E. Lothian	63
Newent ...		SO723260	Glos	143
Northallerton...		SE367942	Yorks	91
North Knapdale ...	Eilean Mor	NR666751	Argyll	58
North Knapdale ...	Keills	NR691806	Argyll	58
Otley ...		SE201453	Yorks	96
Pennant Melangell, see Llangynog				
Riskbuie, see Colonsay				
Rothbury ...		NU058017	Northum	71
Rugby ...		SP593752	Warw	132
Ruthwell ...		NY100670	Dumfrie	75
St. Andrews ...		NO510160	Fife	56
Sandbach ...		SJ760610	Cheshire	110
Sheffield ...		SK354874	Yorks	102
Stamfordham ...		NZ076720	Northum	77
Stapleford ...		SK483373	Notts	121
Thornhill...	Nith Bridge	NX876954	Dumfrie	74
Tynninghame...		NT610791	E. Lothian	63
Wirksworth ...		SK287538	Derby	111
Wolverhampton ...	St. Peter's Church	SO917987	Staf	130

Left table

PICTISH SYMBOL STONES—(Continued)

Parish	Distinctive Name	Grid Reference	County	One-inch Sheet No.
Commonside, Teviothead, see Roberton, and Borthwick Mains				
Congash, see Abernethy and Kincardine				
Corrachree House, see Tarland				
Corskie, Nether, see Cluny				
Craigmyle, see Kincardine O'Neil				
Craigton, see Golspie				
Craw Stone, see Rhynie				
Crichie, see Kintore				
Cromdale, Inverallan and Advie	Findlarig	NH994454	Moray	38
Cromdale, Inverallan and Advie	Cnoc an Fruich	NJ049288	Moray	38
Culsalmond	Newton House	NJ664295	Aber	40
Daviot	Newton of Mounie	NJ759288	Aber	40
Dingwall	...	NH549589	Ross & Crom	27
Dinnacair, see Dunnottar				
Drainie	Kinneddar	NJ223696	Moray	29
Drumblade	Dummuies	NJ558376	Aber	30
Drumbuie, see Urquhart and Glenmoriston				
Drumoak	Park House	NO790980	Aber	40
Drummuies, see Inverurie				
Duffus	Easterton of Roseisle	NJ149691	Moray	29
Duirinish	Tobar na Maor, Colbost	NG200490	Inner Heb	24
Dummuies, see Drumblade				
Dunachton, see Alvie				
Dunnichen	...	NO508488	Angus	50
Dunnottar (6)	Dinnacair	NO888846	Kincar	43
Dunrobin, see Golspie				
Dunrossness	St. Ninian's Isle	HU369209	Shetland	4
Dunrossness (6)	Jarlshof stone disc	HU398096	Shetland	4
Duthill and Rothiemurchus	Lynchurn	NH951206	Inver	38
Dyce	...	NJ875154	Aber	40
Easterton of Roseisle, see Duffus				
Edderton	Clach Biorach	NH709851	Ross & Crom	22
Edinburgh	Prince's Street gardens	NT252736	Midloth	62
Elgan	Upper Manbreen	NJ185376	Moray	29
Evie and Rendall	Broch of Aikerness	HY383268	Orkney	5
Ferry Links, Little, see Golspie				
Fetterangus	...	NJ987508	Aber	31
Findlarig, see Cromdale				
Firth	Broch of Redland	HY379170	Orkney	6
Fiscavaig, see Bracadale				
Forfar	Baggerton	NO470537	Angus	57
Formaston, see Aboyne				
Fyvie (2)	Rothie Brisbane	NJ746378	Aber	30
Fyvie (2)	...	NJ768377	Aber	31
Gairloch	...	NG800771	Ross & Crom	19
Garth, see Birsay and Harray, Knowe of Burrain				
Glenmuick, Tullich and Glengairn	Tullich	NO399975	Aber	42
Golspie	near Dunrobin Castle	NC851007	Suther	15

Right table

Parish	Distinctive Name	Grid Reference	County	One-inch Sheet No.
Golspie	Craigton	NH787983	Suther	15
Golspie	...	NC835001	Suther	15
Golspie (4)	Little Ferry Links	NH814965	Suther	15
Greens, see St. Andrews'				
Huntly	North Redhill	NJ560464	Banff	30
Huntly	Market Place	NJ529399	Aber	30
Inchyra House, see St. Madoes				
Insch	Picardy Stone	NJ610302	Aber	39
Inverallan	...	NJ026260	Moray	38
Inveravon (3)	...	NJ183376	Banff	29
Invereen, see Moy and Dalaro				
Inverkeilor	Kinblethmont House	NO638473	Angus	50
Inverness and Bona	Boar's Stone	NH655412	Inver	28
Inverurie (4)	Kirkyard	NJ780206	Aber	40
Inverurie	Drummuies	NJ742235	Aber	40
†Inverurie	Brandsbutt	NJ761225	Aber	40
Inverurie	Keith Hall, Caskie Ben	NJ779201	Aber	40
Keillor, see Kettins				
Keiss, see Wick				
Keith Hall, see Inverurie				
Kennethmont	Ardlair	NJ557282	Aber	39
Kettins	Keillor	NO273398	Angus	49
Kilrenny	Caiplie Caves	NO599058	Fife	56
Kinblethmont House, see Inverkeilor				
Kincardine O'Neil	Craigmyle	NJ640024	Aber	39
Kinneddar, see Drainie				
Kinellar	Kirkton	NJ821144	Aber	40
Kintradwell, see Loth				
Kintore	Crichie	NJ779197	Aber	40
Kintore	Kirkyard	NJ793163	Aber	40
Kintore (2)	Castle Hill	NJ793163	Aber	40
Kirkmichael	Balnellan	NJ149259	Banff	38
Kirkton, see Kinellar				
Knockando (2)	Pulovenan	NJ202423	Moray	29
Latheron	Latheron Mains	ND193334	Caithness	16
†Latheron	...	ND200336	Caithness	16
Lerwick	...	HU470410	Shetland	3
Leslie	Newbigging of Leslie	NJ604258	Aber	39
Lindores, see Abdie				
Little Ferry Links, see Golspie				
Logie Elphinstone, see Chapel of Garioch				
Loth (4)	Kintradwell	NC930080	Suther	15
Lybster, see Reay				
Lynchurn, see Duthill and Rothiemurchus				
Manbreen, Upper, see Elgan				
Mar Coldstone	Tom a Char	NJ430048	Aber	39
Monifieth	Carn Greg	NO465337	Angus	50
Mortlach	...	NJ323392	Banff	29
Moy and Dalaro	Invereen	NH798315	Inver	28
Nether Corskie, see Cluny				
Newton Corskie, see Culsalmond				
Newton House, see Culsalmond				
Newton of Lewesk, see Rayne				
North Redhill, see Huntly				

PICTISH SYMBOL STONES—(Continued)

Parish	Distinctive Name	Grid Reference	County	One-inch Sheet No.
Old Deer ...	Abbey	NJ969481 ...	Aber ...	31
Pabbay, *see* Barra				
Park House, *see* Drumoak				
Percylieu, *see* Clatt				
Peterhead Farm, *see* Blackford				
Picardy Stone, *see* Insch				
Portree (2) ...	Raasay ...	NG540360 ...	Inner Heb ...	25
Pulovenan, *see* Knockando				
Raasay, *see* Portree				
Rayne ...	Newton of Lewesk ...	NJ694280 ...	Aber ...	40
Reay ...	St. Mary, Lybster ...	ND025701 ...	Caithness ...	11
Reay ...	Sandside, Knock Stanger ...	NC960654 ...	Caithness ...	11
Redhill, North, *see* Huntly				
Redland, Broch of, *see* Firth				
Rhynie (2) ...	Kirkyard ...	NJ499266 ...	Aber ...	39
Rhynie (2) ...	middle of village ...	NJ490263 ...	Aber ...	39
Rhynie... ...	Mains of Rhynie... ...	NJ490263 ...	Aber ...	39
Rhynie... ...	Craw Stone ...	NJ490263 ...	Aber ...	39
Roberton ...	Borthwick Mains ...	NT437140 ...	Roxb ...	69
Roskeen, *see* Alness				
Rothie Brisbane, *see* Fyvie				
St. Andrews ...	Greens	HY542031 ...	Orkney ...	6
†St. Madoes ...	Inchyra House ...	NO191213 ...	Perth ...	55
St. Ninian's Isle, *see* Dunrossness				
Sandness, *see* Walls and Sandness				
Sandside, *see* Reay				
Snizort ...	Clach Ard ...	NG421491 ...	Inner Heb ...	24
South Ronaldsay ...	St. Peter's Kirk ...	ND449931 ...	Orkney ...	7
Strathmartine ...	south-east of castle ...	NO374362 ...	Angus ...	50
Strathmartine ...		NO279353 ...	Angus ...	50
Strathpeffer ...	Clach an Tiumpan ...	NH485585 ...	Ross & Crom ...	27
Strome Shunnamal, *see* Benbecula				
Struan, *see* Blair Atholl				
Tarland ...	Corrachree House ...	NJ464047 ...	Aber ...	39
Tillyarmont, *see* Cairnie				
Tobar na Maor, *see* Duirinish				
Tom a Char, *see* Mar Coldstone				
Torgorm, *see* Urquhart and Logie Wester				
Trusty's Hill, *see* Anwoth				
Tullich, *see* Glenmuick				
Turriff		NJ720490 ...	Aber ...	30
Tyrie		NJ930631 ...	Aber ...	31
Upper Manbreen, *see* Elgan				
Urquhart and Glenmoriston (2)	Drumbuie ...	NH510300 ...	Inver ...	27
Urquhart and Logie Wester	Torgorm...	NH559949 ...	Ross & Crom ...	28
Uyea		HU605999 ...	Shetland ...	1
Walls and Sandness	Sandness ...	HU190170 ...	Shetland ...	3
Walton, *see* Ceres				
Whitefield Farm, *see* Cargill				
Wick	Keiss, Birkle Hills ...	ND339384 ...	Caithness ...	16

Parish	Distinctive Name	Grid Reference	County	One-inch Sheet No.
†Wick	Links of Keiss Bay ...	ND339384 ...	Caithness	16

CROSS SLABS WITH PICTISH SYMBOLS (†stone has Ogam inscription)

Parish	Distinctive Name	Grid Reference	County	One-inch Sheet No.
Aberlemno ...	Kirkyard... ...	NO522555 ...	Angus ...	50
Aberlemno ...	quarter-mile north of kirk ...	NO522559 ...	Angus ...	50
Aberlemno ...	Woodwray ...	NO517566 ...	Angus ...	50
Alyth		NO244487 ...	Perth ...	49
Ardlach ...	Glenferness ...	NH930420 ...	Nairn ...	28
Balluderon, *see* Tealing				
Bore Stone, *see* Gask				
Brodie, *see* Dyke and Moy				
Chapel of Garioch ...	Maiden Stone ...	NJ703247 ...	Aber ...	40
Clach a'Charridh, *see* Fearn				
Cossans, *see* Glamis				
Craigton, *see* Golspie				
Dunfallandy, *see* Logierait				
Dyce	Old kirk ...	NJ875154 ...	Aber ...	40
†Dyke and Moy ...	Brodie Castle ...	NH989584 ...	Moray ...	29
Eassie	Kirk ...	NO355474 ...	Angus ...	50
Edderton ...	Kirkyard... ...	NH711846 ...	Ross & Crom ...	22
Elgin	St. Giles' Kirk ...	NJ221630 ...	Moray ...	29
Fearn	Hilton of Cadboll ...	NH870760 ...	Ross & Crom ...	22
Fearn ...	Clach a'Charridh, Shandwick ...	NH865747 ...	Ross & Crom ...	22
Fordoun ...	Chapel of St. Palladius ...	NO726783 ...	Kincar ...	43
Fowlis Wester ...		NN928240 ...	Perth ...	55
Gask	Bore Stone ...	NN973183 ...	Perth ...	55
Gellyburn, *see* Little Dunkeld				
Glamis...	half-mile south-east of kirk ...	NO395466 ...	Angus ...	50
Glamis...	St. Orland's Stone, Cossans ...	NO400500 ...	Angus ...	50
Glamis...	Manse garden ...	NO385468 ...	Angus ...	50
Glenferness, *see* Ardlach				
†Golspie ...	Craigton ...	NH787983 ...	Suther ...	22
Halkirk ...	Skinnet ...	ND132621 ...	Caithness ...	11
Hilton of Cadboll, *see* Fearn				
Inchbrayock, *see* Montrose				
Inchture ...	Rossie Priory ...	NO292308 ...	Perth ...	49
Kingoldrum		NO334550 ...	Angus ...	49
Kirriemuir (2) ...		NO389544 ...	Angus ...	50
Largo		NO419033 ...	Fife ...	56
Little Dunkeld ...	Gellyburn ...	NO094392 ...	Perth ...	49
Logie Coldstone ...	Migvie ...	NJ436068 ...	Aber ...	39
Logierait ...	Dunfallandy ...	NN950560 ...	Perth ...	49
Logierait ...	Junction of Tay and Tummel ...	NN967520 ...	Perth ...	49
Maiden Stone, *see* Chapel of Garioch				
Martin's Stone, *see* Tealing				
Meigle (6) ...		NO286446 ...	Perth ...	49
Migvie, *see* Logie Coldstone				
Monifeith (3) ...	Old kirk ...	NO499325 ...	Angus ...	50
Montrose ...	Inchbrayock ...	NO708567 ...	Angus ...	50
Monymusk		NJ7015 ...	Aber ...	40
Mortlach ...	Kirktown of Mortlach ...	NJ324394 ...	Banff ...	29
Nigg		NH804722 ...	Ross & Crom ...	22

CROSS SLABS WITH PICTISH SYMBOLS—(Continued)

Parish	Distinctive Name	Grid Reference	County	One-inch Sheet No.
Rosemarkie	...	NH737576	Ross & Crom	28
Rossie Priory, *see* Inchture				
St. Madoes	...	NO196212	Perth	55
St. Orland's Stone, *see* Glamis				
St. Vigeans (6)	...	NO638429	Angus	50
†Scoonie	Old kirkyard	NO384018	Fife	56
Shandwick, *see* Fearn				
Skinnet, *see* Halkirk				
Strathmartine (4)	Old kirkyard	NO378352	Angus	50
Tarbat	...	NH915840	Ross & Crom	22
Tealing	Balluderon	NO374375	Angus	50
Ulbster, *see* Wick				
Wick	St. Martin's, Ulbster	ND336419	Caithness	16
Woodwray, *see* Aberlemno				

CROSS SLABS WITHOUT PICTISH SYMBOLS

Parish	Distinctive Name	Grid Reference	County	One-inch Sheet No.
Aboyne	Loch Kinnord	NO525989	Aber	42
Birsay	...	HY239286	Orkney	6
Bressay	...	HU494410	Shetland	3
Collieburn	...	NC930080	Suther	15
Crieff	...	NN860210	Perth	54
Farr	...	NC714623	Suther	10
Papil	...	HU368316	Shetland	4

PICTISH SYMBOLS IN CAVES

Parish	Distinctive Name	Grid Reference	County	One-inch Sheet No.
Caiplie, *see* Kilrenny				
Covesea, *see* Drainie				
Drainie	Covesea	NJ190710	Moray	29
East Wemyss	The Glass Cave	NT334918	Fife	56
	Court Cave	NT342969	Fife	56
	Doocot Cave	NT343970	Fife	56
	Jonathan's Cave	NT344971	Fife	56
	Cat Cave	NT345972	Fife	56
Kilrenny	Caiplie Caves	NO599058	Fife	56

PICTISH ANIMAL SYMBOLS

Parish	Distinctive Name	Grid Reference	County	One-inch Sheet No.
Burghead	...	NJ109690	Moray	29
Dores	Clune Farm, Dores	NH600350	Inver	28
Falkland	East Lomond Hill	NO244062	Fife	55
Inverness	Kingsmills	NH6643	Inver	28
Inverness	...	NH6648	Inver	28
Kilmichael Glassary	Dunadd	NR837935	Argyll	52
Roskeen	Stittenham	NH644743	Ross & Crom	22
Roskeen	...	NH644743	Ross & Crom	22

PICTISH OGAMS

Parish	Distinctive Name	Grid Reference	County	One-inch Sheet No.
Abernethy	...	NO190164	Perth	55
Aboyne	Formaston	NO570980	Aber	39
Altyre House, *see* Duffus				
Auquhollie, *see* Fetteresso				
Birsay	Beach find	HY235285	Orkney	6
Bressay	...	HU500400	Shetland	3
Brodie Castle, *see* Dyke and Moy				
Burrian, Broch of, *see* North Ronaldsay				
Chapel of Garioch	Logie Elphinstone	NJ703258	Aber	40
Culsalmond	The Newton Stone	NJ664295	Aber	40
Cunningsburgh (3)	Chapel Mail	HU432280	Shetland	4
Duffus	Altyre House	NJ034545	Moray	29
Dunadd, *see* Kilmichael Glassary				
Dunrossness	St. Ninian's Isle	HU366206	Shetland	4
Dyke and Moy	Brodie Castle	NH989584	Moray	29
Evie and Rendall	Broch of Gurness	HY383268	Orkney	6
Fetteresso	Auquhollie Farm	NO823908	Kincard	40
Golspie	Craigton	NH787983	Suther	22
Gurness, Broch of, *see* Evie and Rendall				
Inchyra House, *see* St. Madoes				
Inverurie	Brandsbutt	NJ761225	Aber	40
Keiss, *see* Wick				
Kilmichael Glassary	Dunadd	NR837936	Argyll	52
Latheron	...	ND200336	Caithness	16
Logie Elphinstone, *see* Chapel of Garioch				
Lunnasting, *see* Nesting				
Nesting	Lunnasting	HU480650	Shetland	2
Newton Stone, *see* Culsalmond				
North Ronaldsay	Broch of Burrian	HY763514	Orkney	5
North Uist	Bac Mhic Connain	NF771762	Inver	17
St. Madoes	Inchyra House	NO191213	Perth	55
St. Ninian's Isle, *see* Dunrossness				
Scoonie	...	NO384018	Fife	56
Whiteness	...	HU386444	Shetland	3
Wick	Keiss Bay	ND339584	Caithness	16

PICTISH DOUBLE-LINKED SILVER CHAINS (‡ *carries Pictish symbol*)

Parish	Distinctive Name	Grid Reference	County	One-inch Sheet No.
Abbey St. Bathans	Hordwheel	NT789600	Berwick	63
Caledonian Canal, *see* Inverness				
‡Crawfordjohn	Whitecleugh, Shieldsholm	NS824196	Lanark	68
Edinburgh	Queen's Park, Holyrood	NT2773	Midloth	62
Greenlaw	Herit's Dyke	NT695480	Berwick	63
Haddington	...	NT515739	E. Lothian	63
Holyrood, *see* Edinburgh				
Hordwheel, *see* Abbey St. Bathans				
Inverness	Caledonian Canal	Unlocated	Inver	28
Lauder	...	NT499478	Berwick	62
New Machar	Parkhill	NJ898140	Aber	40

PICTISH DOUBLE-LINKED SILVER CHAINS—(Continued)

Parish	Distinctive Name	Grid Reference	County	One-inch Sheet No.
Nigg		NJ946031 ...	Kincar ...	40
‡Penpont	Drumlanrig Castle ...	NX851993 ...	Dumfrie ...	68
Prestonkirk ...	Traprain Law ...	NT583747 ...	E. Lothian ...	63
Traprain Law, *see* Prestonkirk				
Walston	Walston Borland Farm ...	NT062462 ...	Lanark ...	61
West Linton		Unlocated ...	Peebles ...	62

IMPORTED MEDITERRANEAN POTTERY

Parish	Distinctive Name	Grid Reference	County	One-inch Sheet No.
Abergele St. George ...	Dinorben ...	SH967575 ...	Denb ...	108
Bantham, *see* Thurlestone				
Beddgelert	Dinas Emrys ...	SH606492 ...	Caern ...	107
Cadbury Camp, *see* Yatton				
Cadbury Castle, *see* South Cadbury				
Castle Dore, *see* St. Sampson				
Catterick		SE226990 ...	Yorks ...	91
Cheardach Mhor, *see* South Uist				
Chun Castle, *see* Morvah				
Colvend and Southwick	Mote of Mark ...	NX844541 ...	Kirkcud ...	92
Constantine Bay, *see* St. Merryn				
Coygan Cave, *see* Llanddowror				
Dinas Emrys, *see* Beddgelert				
Dinas Powys, *see* Michaelston le Pit				
Dinorben, *see* Abergele St. George				
Dunadd, *see* Kilmichael Glassary				
Elie		NO490000 ...	Fife ...	68
Godrevy Towans, *see* Gwithian				
Goodrich		SO575196 ...	Here ...	142
Gwithian	Godrevy Towans ...	SW585422 ...	Cornwall ...	189
Hellesvean, *see* St. Ives				
High Peak, *see* Otterton				
Holbeton	Mothecombe ...	SX611473 ...	Devon ...	187
Kilmichael Glassary ...	Dunadd ...	NR837935 ...	Argyll ...	65
Llanddowror	Coygan Cave ...	SN284992 ...	Carm ...	152
Looe	Looe Island ...	SX257515 ...	Cornwall ...	186
Lundy	Lundy Island ...	SS130440 ...	Devon ...	163
Mawgan Porth, *see* St. Mawgan				
Michaelston le Pit ...	Dinas Powys ...	ST148722 ...	Glam ...	154
Monmouth	Brook Housing Estate ...	SO502122 ...	Monm ...	142
Morvah	Chun Castle ...	SW405339 ...	Cornwall ...	189

Parish	Distinctive Name	Grid Reference	County	One-inch Sheet No.
Mote of Mark, *see* Colvend and Southwick				
Otterton	High Peak ...	SY103859 ...	Devon ...	176
Padstow		SW919754 ...	Cornwall ...	185
Penally	Longbury Bank Cave ...	SS112999 ...	Pemb ...	152
Porthmeor, *see* Zennor				
St. Ives	Hellesvean ...	SW505400 ...	Cornwall ...	189
St. Keverne	Trebarveth ...	SW794200 ...	Cornwall ...	190
St. Mawgan	Mawgan Porth ...	SW854672 ...	Cornwall ...	185
St. Merryn	Constantine Bay ...	SW860750 ...	Cornwall ...	185
St. Sampson	Castle Dore ...	SX104548 ...	Cornwall ...	186
South Cadbury ...	Cadbury Castle ...	ST628252 ...	Somerset ...	166
South Uist	a Cheardach Mhor ...	NF770420 ...	Outer Heb	23
Tean, *see* Tresco				
Thurlestone	Bantham ...	SX663437 ...	Devon ...	187
Tintagel		SX030890 ...	Cornwall ...	185
Trebarveth, *see* St. Keverne				
Tresco	Tean ...	SV908165 ...	I. of Scilly	189
Yatton	Cadbury Camp ...	ST440650 ...	Somerset ...	156
Zennor	Porthmeor ...	SW439372 ...	Cornwall ...	189

FRANKISH - GAULISH WARE

Parish	Distinctive Name	Grid Reference	County	One-inch Sheet No.
Bantham, *see* Thurlestone				
Buston, *see* Dreghorn				
Colvend and Southwick	Mote of Mark	NX844541 ...	Kirkcud ...	92
Dinas Powys, *see* Michaelston le Pit				
Dreghorn	Buston crannog ...	NS415435 ...	Ayrshire ...	60
Dunadd, *see* Kilmichael Glassary				
Gwithian	Godrevy Towans	SW585422 ...	Cornwall ...	189
Hellesvean, *see* St. Ives				
Kilmichael Glassary ...	Dunadd ...	NR837935 ...	Argyll ...	65
Largo		NO423035 ...	Fife ...	56
Lochlee, *see* Tarbolton				
Michaelston le Pit ...	Dinas Powys ...	ST148722 ...	Glam ...	154
Mote of Mark, *see* Colvend and Southwick				
St. Ives	Hellesvean ...	SW505400 ...	Cornwall ...	189
Stevenston		NS265421 ...	Ayrshire ...	59
Tarbolton	Lochlee crannog	NS454301 ...	Ayrshire ...	67
Tean, *see* Tresco				
Thurlestone	Bantham ...	SX663437 ...	Devon ...	187
Tresco	Tean ...	SV908165 ...	I. of Scilly	189

ONE-INCH SEVENTH SERIES

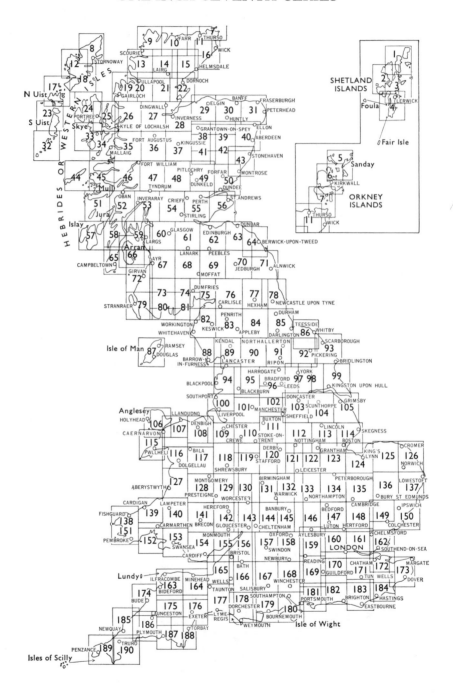

THE NATIONAL GRID REFERENCE SYSTEM
OF GREAT BRITAIN

Diagram showing 100 km. squares and the letters used to designate them

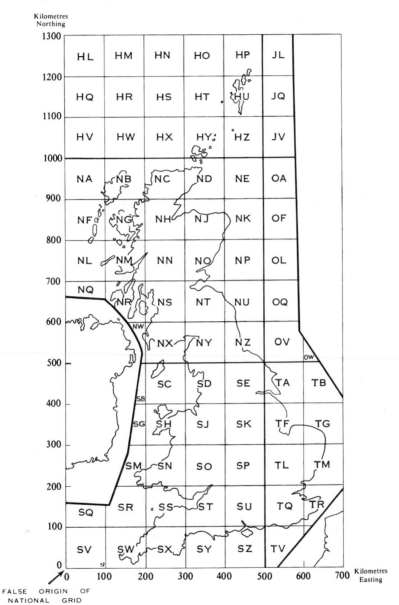

FALSE ORIGIN OF
NATIONAL GRID

4000/74